i Think: it's Elementary!

America's Government

by Kendra Corr

With contributions by Wendy Moeller

© InspirEd Educators, Inc.   Atlanta, Georgia

** It is the goal of InspirEd Educators to create instructional materials that are interesting, engaging, and challenging. Our student-centered approach incorporates both content and skills, placing particular emphasis on reading, writing, vocabulary development, and critical and creative thinking in the content areas.

Edited by Sharon Coletti and Amy Hellen

Cover graphics by Sharon Coletti and Print1 Direct

Copyright © 2010 by InspirEd Educators, Inc.

ISBN # 978-1-933558-87-5

** FOR INDIVIDUAL TEACHER / PARENT USE **

Printed in the United States of America

About InspirEd Educators

InspirEd Educators was founded in 2000 by author Sharon Coletti. Our mission is to provide interesting, student-centered, and thought-provoking instructional materials. To accomplish this, we design lesson plans with standards-based content information presented in a variety of ways and used as the vehicle for developing critical and creative thinking, reading, writing, collaboration, problem-solving, and other necessary and enduring skills. By requiring students to THINK, our lessons ensure FAR greater retention than simple memorization of facts!

Initially our company offered large, comprehensive, multi-disciplinary social studies curricula. Then in 2008 we joined forces with another small company and author, Kendra Corr, and launched our second line of "I Think: Thematic Units," which we've been expanding ever since. These flexible and affordable resources are ideal for individual, small, or large-group instruction. We hope you will find our company's unique approach valuable and that we can serve you again in the near future.

If you are interested in our other offerings, you can find information on our main website at **www.inspirededucators.com**.

InspirEd Educators materials provide engaging lesson plans that vary daily and include:

- Lesson-specific Springboards (warm-ups)
- Writing activities
- Critical and creative thinking
- Problem-solving
- Test-taking skill development
- Primary source analyses (DBQ's)
- Multiple perspectives
- Graphic analyses
- Fascinating readings
- Simulations
- Story-telling
- Practical use of technology
- Debates
- Plays
- Research
- Graphic organizers
- AND SO MUCH MORE!!!!!

Thank you for choosing our units,
Sharon Coletti, President
InspirEd Educators

Tips for Teaching with this InspirEd Unit

- Before beginning the unit, take time to look through the Objectives and lessons. This will give you a chance to think about what you want to emphasize and decide upon any modifications, connections, or extensions you'd like to include.

- Arrange for your student(s) to have books available or to check them out. A suggested reading list is included, but any books of interest related to the unit subject are fine. We do strongly suggest the reading link to enhance this study! Activities are included that refer to the book(s) being read, and students should be encouraged to discuss any connections throughout.

- Give your student(s) a copy of the Objective page at the beginning of unit study. The Objectives serve as an outline of the content to be covered and provide a means to review information. Have the student(s) define the vocabulary terms as they progress through the lessons and thoroughly answer the essential questions. You can review their responses as you go along or wait and check everything as a test review. It is important that your student(s) have some opportunity to receive feedback on their Objective answers, since assessments provided at the end of the unit are based on these.

- Read through each lesson's materials before beginning. This will help you better understand lesson concepts; decide when and how to present the vocabulary and prepare the handouts (or transparencies) you will need.

- "Terms to know" can be introduced at the beginning of lessons or reviewed at the end, unless specified otherwise. (In a few instances the intent is for students to discover the meanings of the terms.)

- Our materials are intended to prompt discussion. Often students' answers may vary, but it's important that they be able to substantiate their opinions and ideas with facts. Let the discussion flow!

- Note that differentiated assessments are provided at the end of the unit. Feel free to use any of these as appropriate; cut-and-paste to revise, or create your own tests as desired.

- For additional information and research sites refer to the Resource Section in the back of the unit.

- InspirEd Educators units are all about thinking and creativity, so allow yourself the freedom to adapt the materials as you see fit. Our goal is to provide a springboard for you to jump from in your teaching and your student(s)' learning.

- ENJOY! We at InspirEd Educators truly believe that teaching and learning should be enjoyable, so we do our best to make our lessons interesting and varied. We want you and your student(s) to love learning!

TABLE OF CONTENTS

 *Some Suggested Reading*

NOTE: Depending upon ability, have your student(s) read one or more of the following titles (or others as available) on the topic of America's government to accompany this unit study. The final lesson pertains to the chosen book(s).

** Bailey Beard, Darleen, <u>Operation Clean Sweep,</u> Farrar, Straus and Giroux, 2004.

Brindell Fradin, Dennis, <u>Samuel Adams: The Father of American Independence</u>, Clarion Books 1998.

Collier, Christopher, <u>Creating the Constitution: 1787 (Drama of American History)</u>, Marshall Cavendish Children's Books, 1998.

Decarolis, Lisa, <u>Alexander Hamilton: Federalist and Founding Father (Library of American Lives and Times</u>), Rosen Publishing Group, 2003.

Fradin, Dennis Brindell and McCurdy, Michael, <u>The Signers: 56 Stories Behind the Declaration of Independence</u>, Walker Books for Young Readers, 2003.

Freedman, Russell, <u>Give Me Liberty: The Story of the Declaration of Independence</u>, Holiday House, 2002.

* Fritz, Jean, <u>Shh! We're Writing the Constitution</u>, Putnam Juvenile, 1997.

* Fritz, Jean, <u>Will You Sign Here John Hancock</u>? Putnam Juvenile, 1997.

Fritz, Jean, <u>The Great Little Madison (Unforgettable Americans)</u>, Putnam Juvenile, 1998.

Kroll, Steven, <u>Dear Mr. President: John Quincy Adams: Letters from a Southern Planter's Son</u>, Winslow House, 2001.

Krull, Kathleen, <u>A Kid's Guide to America's Bill of Rights: Curfews, Censorship and the 100 Pound Giant</u>, HarperCollins, 1999.

Lawson, Robert, <u>Ben and Me: An Astonishing Life of Benjamin Franklin by His Good Mouse Amos,</u> Little Brown Books for Young Readers, 1988.

Levy, Elizabeth, <u>... If You Were There When They Signed the Constitution</u>, Scholastic Paperbacks, 1992.

 * Maestro, Betsy, <u>A More Perfect Union: The Story of Our Constitution,</u> Collins, 1990.

Morin, Isobel, <u>Politics American Style</u>, 21st Century, 1999.

Pfueger, Linda, <u>Thomas Jefferson: Creating a Nation,</u> Enslow Publishers, 2004.

* * Schwabach, Karen, <u>The Hope Chest</u>, Random House Books for Young Readers, 2008.

Severance, John B. <u>Thomas Jefferson: Architect of Democracy,</u> Clarion Books, 1998.

Thaler, Mike, <u>The Class Election from the Black Lagoon</u>, Turtleback, 2004.

Thomas, Joyce Carol, <u>Linda Brown You are Not Alone: The Brown vs. the Board of Education Decision</u>, Hyperion, 2003.

* Less Challenging

** More Challenging

GOVERNMENT OBJECTIVES

Vocabulary - Be able to define and use the following terms:

- government
- independence
- colonist
- founding fathers
- constitution
- federal
- tax
- legislature
- amend
- convention
- delegate
- representative
- population
- document
- ratify
- popular sovereignty
- preamble
- citizen
- bill
- qualification
- pardon
- treaty
- execute
- veto
- court
- appeal
- violate
- judicial review
- justices
- checks and balances
- summary
- military
- impeach
- amendments
- trial
- jury
- witness
- due process
- political party
- candidate
- environment
- independent
- Electoral College
- elector
- interest group
- acronym
- discrimination
- issue
- tourism
- veteran
- primary source

Fully answer the following questions:

1. Explain why the founding fathers wrote the Declaration of Independence.
2. Explain why the Articles of Confederation were weak.
3. Describe decisions made at the Constitutional Convention.
4. Describe the basics of the U.S. Constitution.
5. Explain what Preamble does.
6. Describe the basic powers of the three branches of the government.
7. Explain the system of checks and balances in the U.S. government.
8. Explain the importance of the first ten Amendments to the Constitution.
9. Explain why the Constitution has an amendment process.
10. Explain what makes a good citizen.
11. Explain the roles of political parties and the Electoral College in elections.
12. Explain the difference between local, state, and federal government.

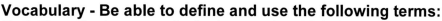

Vocabulary - Be able to define and use the following terms:
Definitions for terms are in the lessons in which they are introduced.

Fully answer the following questions:

1. The Declaration of Independence was written to list the complaints colonists had against the king, state their basic beliefs about government (such as the rights to life, liberty and the pursuit of happiness), and announce that they wanted to separate from England.

2. The Articles of Confederation gave the states too much power and the federal government almost none. There was only one federal branch, a legislature, with no national leadership. There was no way to settle disputes among the states, and neither the size nor populations of states was taken into account.

3. Delegates at the Constitutional Convention met to fix problems in the Articles of Confederation but instead wrote a completely new government plan. They specified many powers of the states and federal governments, decided how people would be represented, and how laws would be made and carried out.

4. The Constitution is a written plan of how our government works. It includes an introduction (the Preamble), a body (that outlines the powers and duties of each of the three branches of government), and amendments (changes in the document).

5. The Preamble states the intent of the Constitution and government: to protect the rights of the people, provide for defense, improve people's lives, and to make the U.S. a good place to live.

6. The Legislature is made up of two houses, the Senate and House of Representatives. Its main job is to make the nation's laws. Additional powers and duties can be found on page 39. The Executive Branch puts the laws into action. Additional powers and duties can be found on page 45. The Judicial Branch handles problems or disagreements that may arise from laws and decides if laws violate any provisions of the Constitution.

7. The powers of the federal government are divided among three branches. These powers can be checked, or stopped by another branch in many cases. This system of checks and balances was established by the founding fathers to ensure no one branch could become too powerful.

8. The first ten amendments are called the Bill of Rights. They state the freedoms and protections of U.S. citizens and guarantee the powers of states. The Bill of Rights includes personal freedoms that apply to all and rights of the accused to due process and equal protection under the law.

9. The Constitution was designed to change with the times. The country was very different when its government was founded. Amendments allow for change, but require 2/3rds of the states to agree. The process prevents too many changes.

10. Acts of good citizenship include voting, obeying the laws, staying informed about events and issues, being involved in community affairs and beyond, serving in the military, serving on juries, and so forth.

11. Political parties are groups of people who share the same ideas about government. Members work and donate money to help their party's candidates be elected and influence government. The Electoral College is a group of people who officially elect the president. The body was created by the founding fathers to protect the presidency at a time when most were uneducated and uninformed. Debate continues as to whether it is still needed.

12. The federal government tends to handle big-picture issues that affect EVERYONE, while state and local governments deal with details that affect the local community or state.

Springboard:
Students should read "The Enlightenment" and answer the questions.

Objective: The student will be able to explain why the Declaration of Independence was written.

Materials:	The Enlightenment (Springboard handout) The Declaration of Independence (handout) Breaking It Down (handout)
Terms to know:	**government** - rule and control of a country **independence** - free from outside control **colonist** - person in America under English rule

Procedure:

· While reviewing the Springboard, make sure the student(s) understand that many ideas for our government came from the Enlightenment. Then explain that _in this lesson the student(s) will study one of the first pieces of writing that led to a new U.S. government – the Declaration of Independence_.

· Distribute "The Declaration of Independence" and "Breaking It Down." (**NOTE:** The text has been simplified and shortened for younger students. Advanced students can read the original text online or in a textbook, if desired.)

· Have the student(s) work independently, in pairs, or small groups to read the document and complete the analysis form.

· Have them share and compare their ideas. If they haven't already studied the American Revolution, make sure the student(s) understand that war did occur between England and the colonies that led to the creation of the United States.

The Enlightenment

The Enlightenment, also known as the "Age of Reason," was a time when people began to look at the world in new ways. Science became a careful study with detailed records kept of all that was seen. As a result, many new discoveries were made in science and medicine. Before this time people could not explain what went on around them. Religion or spirits and monsters were used to explain the world.

Art and writing also changed during the Enlightenment. Many writers and thinkers of the time had strong views about government. Their work focused on the fact that rulers should have to answer to those they ruled. They spoke of fairness and people's rights. They spoke out against kings and queens who grew rich while their people suffered.

Enlightenment ideas spread outside of Europe as well. In the American colonies, leaders read about these new ideas. They began to question the way they were treated by the king. Later many ideas of Enlightenment writers would show up in the United States **documents** such as the Declaration of Independence and the Constitution.

Which definition of the word "document" **BEST FITS** its use in the reading?

    A. a computer file   C. to keep a record

    B. a piece of writing   D. to prove something

Which of these groups of people probably did **NOT** agree with Enlightenment ideas?

    A. kings   C. scientists

    B. citizens   D. writers

A "main idea" is a sentence that sums up all of the information given. Which sentence BEST states the main idea of the passage?

    A. The Enlightenment was also called the Age of Reason.

    B. There were more scientists during the Enlightenment.

    C. The Constitution was written during the Enlightenment.

    D. The Enlightenment was important to the United States.

The Enlightenment led people in America to fight for their freedom. So do you think it was a good thing or not? Why? _____

_____

_____

_____

_____

The Enlightenment, also known as the "Age of Reason," was a time when people began to look at the world in new ways. Science became a careful study with detailed records kept of all that was seen. As a result, many new discoveries were made in science and medicine. Before this time people could not explain what went on around them. Religion or spirits and monsters were used to explain the world.

Art and writing also changed during the Enlightenment. Many writers and thinkers of the time had strong views about government. Their work focused on the fact that rulers should have to answer to those they ruled. They spoke of fairness and people's rights. They spoke out against kings and queens who grew rich while their people suffered.

Enlightenment ideas spread outside of Europe as well. In the American colonies, leaders read about these new ideas. They began to question the way they were treated by the king. Later many ideas of Enlightenment writers would show up in the United States **documents** such as the Declaration of Independence and the Constitution.

Which definition of the word "document" **BEST FITS** its use in the reading?

    A. a computer file   C. to keep a record

    B. a piece of writing *   D. to prove something

(The passage refers to the Declaration of Independence and Constitution as "documents," which students should know are written works.)

Which of these groups of people probably did **NOT** agree with Enlightenment ideas?

    A. kings *   B. citizens   C. scientists   D. writers

(Enlightenment writers challenged the power and behavior of kings and queens, therefore it is likely they would not have agreed with these ideas.)

A "main idea" is a sentence that sums up all of the information given. Which sentence BEST states the main idea of the passage?

    A. The Enlightenment was also called the Age of Reason.

    B. There were more scientists during the Enlightenment.

    C. The Constitution was written during the Enlightenment.

    D. The Enlightenment was important to the United States.*

(Choice A is a detail and there is not enough information to support Choices B or C. The point of the passage is that the new ideas were very influential on those who wrote our founding documents.)

The Enlightenment led people in America to fight for their freedom. So do you think it was a good thing or not? Why? *Answers will vary, but should be supported.*

The Declaration of Independence In Simple Terms

In Congress, July 4, 1776.
Declaration of the thirteen United States of America.

There are times when one group of people needs to break away from the nation ruling it to become a free country. When this happens, the people should explain their actions.

We believe these things to be true: All men are equal and have certain rights that cannot be taken away by anyone else. These rights are the right to life, liberty, and the pursuit of happiness. When a government or ruler tries to stand in the way of these rights, the people should be able to get rid of that government and set up their own. In these colonies, we have been treated very poorly by England. Here are the things that have been done to us by the king:

- The king will not let us pass laws for the good of everyone.
- He calls men together to make laws when we cannot be there.
- He won't let the colonists take over land from the Native Americans.
- He won't let us choose our own judges.
- He makes us pay for officials that we don't want.
- He forces us to provide housing for his soldiers.
- He won't let us buy and sell with whom we want.
- He makes us buy and sell only with England.
- He forces us to pay taxes in which we had no say.
- He sends people accused of crimes to England for their trials.
- He encourages people to cause problems in the colonies.

We have asked him to stop many times but he has not. We have tried to ask others in England to hear our case, but they will not. So, we must now break from England. We hope we can stay friends with the English but if not, we will fight them as enemies in the war.

We think God will view our actions as right; to declare the United States as now free from the rule of the King of England. As a free country, the United States of America now has the right to declare war, to make peace, and to join with other countries as friends, just as other free nations do. We will fight for our freedom with the help of God. All this we promise on our lives, our property, and our honor.

BREAKING IT DOWN

DIRECTIONS: Use the document information to complete the organizer.

WHY was this document written?	What do the authors BELIEVE?
What HAPPENED that led to the writing of this document?	**What is likely to happen NEXT?**

Based on the information given, what do you think is meant by these rights?

Life: _____

_____

_____

_____

Liberty: _____

_____

_____

_____

Pursuit of happiness:_____

_____

_____

_____

DIRECTIONS: Use the document information to complete the organizer.

WHY was this document written?	What do the authors BELIEVE?
The document was written to announce that the colonies intended to separate from England. The authors and signers thought it was necessary to explain why they were taking these actions. The document then goes on to list several reasons (the original document lists 27 complaints!) why they are declaring independence.	*The authors believe that all men have certain rights that cannot be taken away by a ruler or government. They also believe that people have the right to break away if they are treated unfairly.*
What HAPPENED that led to the writing of this document? *The King of England treated the colonists very unfairly in their opinion. (Students can also list the specific complaints in the document.)* *The authors also state that they tried to reason with the king and other Englishmen to no avail.*	What is likely to happen NEXT? *The authors make it clear that they are willing to go to war to gain their freedom from England. They swear on their property and honor that they will fight for these things they believe in. Even if students do not realize that this document was written shortly after the American Revolution began, they should be able to reason that the document is likely to lead to conflict with the king!*

Based on the information given, what do you think is meant by these rights?

Life: *Answers will vary but should be supported by information from the lesson. In general, this right refers to people being able to live without fear of unlawful imprisonment, torture, or other mistreatment. One important role of government is to protect its citizens. Police and soldiers are used to protect people from harm within the nation or outside.*

Liberty: *Answers will vary but should be supported by information from the lesson. Enlightenment writings emphasized the importance of freedom. Freedom of speech, freedom of religion, expression, etc. are all included among personal liberties.*

Pursuit of happiness: *Answers will vary but should be supported by information from the lesson. People in America have a great deal of personal freedom, which ends at the point that individual freedoms restrict the rights of others. No one, individual or in the government, has the right to prevent another from pursuing happiness.*

Nice Try!

Springboard:
Students should read "The Articles of Confederation"
and answer the questions.

Objective: The student will be able to explain some key reasons why the Articles of Confederation were too weak to govern the nation.

Materials: The Articles of Confederation (Springboard handout)
Capitol Beat (3-page handout)
Pointing Out Problems (handout)

Terms to know: **founding fathers** - leaders of early American history
constitution - plan for a government
federal - for the whole nation
tax - money paid to a government
legislature - body of law makers
amend - change or add to, as a law

Procedure:

- After reviewing the Springboard, explain that *in this lesson the student(s) will learn about some of the problems of governing the United States under the Articles of Confederation*.

- Distribute the "Capitol Beat" skit. **For group instruction** have students read the play in groups of three or choose three students to perform it. **For individualized instruction** the parent / teacher should read the play with the student combining the two "expert" parts.

- Then distribute "Pointing Out Problems" and have the student(s) complete the analysis form individually, in pairs, or groups.

- Have them share / compare answers. (*Revision ideas will vary, but lists of weaknesses should include the following:*
  ○ *The states had too much power; the federal government was weaker than the states.*
  ○ *There was no federal court system or president; only a legislature (no separation of powers)*
  ○ *Only the states could impose taxes; the federal government had no way to raise money to pay debts, raise armies, or other needs.*
  ○ *It took 9 of 13 states to agree on laws and other business and required unanimous consent to amend the Articles.*
  ○ *There was no way to settle disputes among the states.*
  ○ *There was no national leader! There were only disagreeing states.*
  ○ *States of differing size and needs could not come together to decide things; decision-making was slow and nearly impossible.*)

The Articles of Confederation

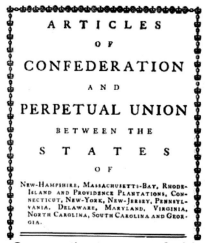

After the Declaration of Independence was signed in 1776, the founding fathers met again right away. They had to form a government to rule the new nation during the war and after being freed from England. So they set to work and wrote the Articles of Confederation. That document became the first "constitution" in 1781 when all thirteen states signed it.

It took almost five years to get the Articles of Confederation approved by the states. Some states were afraid they would not have a fair say. Small states such as Delaware and Connecticut were afraid they would play too small a role in the nation's government. Larger states like Pennsylvania and North Carolina feared they would have to pay to support the government more than the smaller states. In general, the Articles of Confederation gave the states many powers.

The founding fathers had other concerns, too. They wanted a weak federal government. They didn't like the way England ruled the colonies, so they didn't want a king. They wanted things to be different than in the past. So instead of forming a strong government to join the thirteen states, they built "a firm league of friendship" among them. The federal government was given very little power over the states.

The new government held together long enough to fight and win the American Revolution. But after the war, it soon became clear that a stronger government was needed.

What were the writers of the Articles of Confederation thinking when they formed the new government?

Why do you think their task was so hard?

What problems do you think a weak federal government could cause?

The Articles of Confederation - Suggested Answers

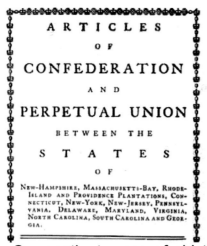

ARTICLES
OF
CONFEDERATION
AND
PERPETUAL UNION
BETWEEN THE
STATES
OF
New-Hampshire, Massachusetts-Bay, Rhode-Island and Providence Plantations, Connecticut, New-York, New-Jersey, Pennsylvania, Delaware, Maryland, Virginia, North Carolina, South Carolina and Georgia.

After the Declaration of Independence was signed in 1776, the founding fathers met again right away. They had to form a government to rule the new nation during the war and after being freed from England. So they set to work and wrote the Articles of Confederation. That document became the first "constitution" in 1781 when all thirteen states signed it.

It took almost five years to get the Articles of Confederation approved by the states. Some states were afraid they would not have a fair say. Small states such as Delaware and Connecticut were afraid they would play too small a role in the nation's government. Larger states like Pennsylvania and North Carolina feared they would have to pay to support the government more than the smaller states. In general, the Articles of Confederation gave the states many powers.

The founding fathers had other concerns, too. They wanted a weak federal government. They didn't like the way England ruled the colonies, so they didn't want a king. They wanted things to be different than in the past. So instead of forming a strong government to join the thirteen states, they built "a firm league of friendship" among them. The federal government was given very little power over the states.

The new government held together long enough to fight and win the American Revolution. But after the war, it soon became clear that a stronger government was needed.

What were the writers of the Articles of Confederation thinking when they formed the new government?
- *Small states were afraid their "voices" would not be heard in a federal government. They very much feared the effects that NOT having an equal say in government would have.*
- *concerns of the large states that they would have to pay an unfair amount*
- *fears about a powerful federal government*

Why do you think their task was so hard?
Answers will vary somewhat, but students should recognize that trying to address everyone's concerns would be a challenge. Trying to form a government that would be strong enough to take care of things without being too powerful, one that met the needs of large states, as well as small ones, and to please everyone was a HUGE task!

What problems do you think a weak federal government could cause?
Answers may vary and may include: states disagreeing about who has the power to make decisions; solving problems between the states; bringing new states into the nation; paying to protect the country; agreeing on taxes; slow process of making decisions; difficulty agreeing on anything, etc.

# Capitol Beat

Characters: *Az Kweschin, Capitol Beat Host*
Adora Thepast, American History Professor
Imen Ekspert, American Government Expert

Az: Good evening ladies and gentlemen and welcome to this edition of Capitol Beat. We are very pleased to have a special guest with us tonight. Please give a warm welcome to *Adora Thepast*. Mr./Ms. Thepast is an expert in U.S. History. He/She teaches at Georgetown University right here in Washington, D.C.

Adora: Thank you, Az. I am most pleased to be here.

Az: And, we are also thrilled to have an American government expert with us. Please welcome *Imen Ekspert*.

Imen: Thank you for having me Alice!

Az: Of course. Now, we have asked the two of you here to talk about the very early history of America.

Adora: That's right. Do you know, Az, most people think the U.S. government was formed by the U.S. Constitution?

Az: Is that not true? I always thought that was the case.

Imen: Well it is true, but it's also false. Our government WAS formed by the Constitution, but there was another government before that. There was another document called the Articles of Confederation that governed the young land.

Az: (*shocked*) Really?!?

Adora: Yes, the Articles were written soon after the colonists declared themselves free of England. They formed the first U.S. government.

Az: That's interesting. Why then, have most people never heard of these Articles?

Adora: Well, they didn't last long and didn't work very well. After a few years they were thrown out. That's when the founding fathers wrote the Constitution.

Imen: That is true, but I think we're getting ahead of ourselves.

Az: Let's talk about these Articles a bit. Imen, can you please tell us about them?

Imen: I'd be glad to. The Articles of Confederation joined the thirteen states into a loose group to work together. The writers wanted the states to have most of the power in the country.

Az: Why?

Imen: Everyone at the time was very upset about the way the King of England had treated the colonies. They didn't want some strong leader or leaders telling them what to do.

Az: That makes sense. The colonists, after all, had fought a bloody war to break away from the king.

Imen: Indeed! And each state saw itself as different and apart from the others. People spoke of themselves as Virginians or New Yorkers. No one said, "I'm an American."

Adora: Imen makes a good point; the states did not want to answer to anyone.

Az: So what did the Articles of Confederation say?

Adora: Well, as Imen noted, most powers were given to the states. States could collect taxes from people. And each state had its own courts to try people and settle problems. Then, any laws the U.S. did pass had to be enforced by the states.

Az: It sounds like the states did just about everything!

Adora: They did. The federal, or national government, had little to do.

Az: Did they do anything?

Imen: Not a great deal. The federal government had only one branch – a legislature. It could make laws but it had no way of making sure anyone followed them.

Az: What about a president?

Adora: There was no president or courts; only a legislature.

Az: So this legislature must have been busy, doing the job three branches do now?

Imen: But the government wasn't busy at all. I mean it did have the power to set up a post office.

Az: That's it?!?

Adora: No there's more. The federal government could declare war and make agreements with other nations. They could also name officers to the army and navy…

Imen: Yes, they could do all of those things. But then almost anything they did had to be approved by the states.

Az: What do you mean?

Imen: You see the national government didn't have the power to tax. They could raise an army, but had to ask the states for money to do so. Being able to declare a war without having the money to fight it meant almost nothing.

Adora: So true, Imen. The federal government had no way to pay for things. After the war, the U.S. owed money it borrowed to fight, but had no way to repay it.

Az: That does sound like a problem. I'm sure that wasn't the only one though.

Imen: Not at all. Any time the federal government wanted to do anything, it had to get nine out of thirteen states to approve. They couldn't pass laws or get money or solve problems among states. It was all so difficult. The states were so different and had such different needs. They just couldn't agree on much!

Adora: It was even worse if they wanted to amend the Articles. To make changes all thirteen states had to agree!

Az: I would imagine that would be tough. It's hard to get thirteen people to agree on something, much less thirteen states!

Imen: Which leads us to another weakness of the Articles of Confederation. The federal government had no way to settle problems that came up among the states.

Az: What kinds of problems?

Adora: Well, for one thing, if two states wanted to trade but could not work out an agreement, the federal government had no power to help. Each state had its own court systems and laws.

Az: So who had the final say? Which states got their way? The biggest ones?

Imen: Sometimes. Think of that first government as thirteen countries trying to live as one. They rarely agreed on any actions. It was a real mess.

Adora: One other point to make Az, if I could.

Az: Please go on.

Adora: I know we said this before, but it is worth noting again. It is important to keep in mind that all of the governing rested in one branch of government – the legislature.

Az: I remember, but why is that such a big deal?

Adora: One reason our federal government has worked so well for so long is that power is divided. One branch makes the laws, one carries them out, and one settles problems that arise because of those laws.

Imen: Otherwise known as (*makes air quotes*) "separation of powers."

Adora: Yes, you see under the Articles of Confederation there was no leader at all. There was just a legislature with no real power!

Az: I see. So what was the point of even having a federal government?

Imen: Quite the point; and one of the many reasons the Articles had to be changed. The Constitution was then written to address these problems. It….

Az: I am so sorry Imen, but I'm going to have to stop you there. We are all out of time for this week's show. I want to thank both our guests for a very interesting chat. I hope you all enjoyed our talk and will join us again next week for "Capitol Beat."

POINTING OUT PROBLEMS

DIRECTIONS: List and explain five MAIN problems with the Articles of Confederation. Then make a list of changes you think needed to be made at the bottom of the page.

Problem 1: _____

_____

_____

_____

Problem 2: _____

_____

_____

_____

Problem 3: _____

_____

_____

_____

Problem 4: _____

_____

_____

_____

Problem 5: _____

_____

_____

_____

CHANGES NEEDED:

_____

_____

_____

_____

_____

_____

Meeting of the Minds

Objective: The student will be able to explain some key decisions made at the Constitutional Convention.

Materials:
    Convention Rules (Springboard handout)
    You Are There (cut-out cards)
    Decisions, Decisions (handout)
    Our Government Plan (handout or transparency)

Terms to know:
    convention - a large meeting
    delegate - representative at a convention
    representative - one who speaks/votes for the people
    population - the number of people in a place

Procedure:

- While reviewing the Springboard, point out that *secrecy was very important at the Constitutional Convention. Heavy drapes covered the windows at Independence Hall and the doors were kept locked at all times. In fact notes recorded at the meetings by James Madison were not made public until after his death years later!* Go on to explain that *in this lesson the student(s) will act as delegates to the Constitutional Convention and debate some of the same points discussed all those years ago.*

- **For group instruction** divide the class into three groups approximating the percentages of the three regions on the "Delegate Information" cards. Give each group their card and a "Decisions, Decisions" handout. **For individualized instruction** the student should choose one region and complete the activity individually or with help as needed and then select another region and repeat the activity.

- Allow a few minutes for groups to discuss and complete their decisions and then make the following announcement:
  "As President of the Constitutional Convention, I call this meeting to order. You have had time to discuss your ideas with your state delegations and now it is time to make final decisions. (Hand out or display the "Our Government Plan" page.) When I call upon you, each state should report its ideas. If there are differing opinions on each topic, we shall discuss that point. Then we will vote and record our final decisions on this form."

- Discuss the "Decisions, Decisions" questions and have each group report in their ideas. When conflicts arise, allow each group to present their arguments and then vote on the proposed ideas (majority rules). Once decisions are made, record them on the transparency or handouts.

- Ask the student(s) to predict how similar their ideas were to what was actually decided at the Constitutional Convention. Then explain that *the student(s) will learn what was actually included in the U.S. Constitution in upcoming lessons*.

CONVENTION RULES

By 1786 it was clear the Articles of Confederation were not going to work. A meeting was set for May in Philadelphia, Pennsylvania, to discuss changes. At what came to be called the "Constitutional Convention," fifty-five men from the thirteen states gathered. They originally planned to just fix the Articles, but ended up writing a whole new plan of government. In the first three days of the meeting, they wrote rules for it. Here are some.

DIRECTIONS: Tell why you think each rule was important for the Constitutional Convention.

1. The President of the Convention (in this case, George Washington) will be in charge. He will call on those who want to speak and choose who speaks and in what order. Anyone who wants to speak should address only him.

2. Members are not allowed to talk about what goes on at the convention. All discussed is to be kept secret!

3. Any topic can be brought up again at a later time.

4. Members cannot speak more than twice on the same topic and cannot speak more than once until everyone has a chance to speak first.

5. Every day the minutes (a record of what was said and done) from the day before must be read before any new business takes place.

6. There must be at least seven states represented to do business. If less than seven show up, the meetings for the day must end.

Explain one or two MAIN reasons these rules were written._____
_____
_____
_____
_____

You Are There

You are a delegate from one of the New England states (choose Massachusetts, Connecticut or New Hampshire; Rhode Island did not send any delegates to the convention). You represent about 15% (15 out of 100) of those present to make decisions. Your region is small compared to the other two. Yet New England has a great deal of trade and businesses, especially on the coast of Massachusetts. Your people are well-educated and keep up with events by reading newspapers and books.

You are a delegate from one of the Middle states (choose New York, New Jersey, Pennsylvania or Delaware). Delegates from your region make up about 40% (40 out of 100) of the people at the Philadelphia meeting. Two of your states, New York and Pennsylvania, are very large. Many people live in this region. Your location on the coast means that there is much fishing and trade. Many rich and educated people live in these states.

You are a delegate from one of the Southern states (choose Virginia, Maryland, North Carolina, South Carolina or Georgia). Delegates from your region make up almost 50% (1/2) of the delegates at the convention. While your states have a lot of land, there are far more people in the North. The only state in your region with a large population is Virginia. Virginia was also the first successful colony in America and has many famous leaders from there. Most of the region depends on farming and slaves. There are not many businesses or industries in this region.

Decisions, Decisions

DIRECTIONS: As delegates at the Constitutional Convention, your job is to form a new government. Discuss each question with your group and record your ideas.

1. Should we change the Articles of Confederation or start over? Why?

2. How strong should the federal government be? What powers do you think it should have?

3. What kind of leader should the government have? What powers should he/she have? How can we make sure this leader doesn't get too powerful?

4. How should laws be made? How many votes or states should be needed to pass laws? Who should have to approve them? Why?

5. How many people should represent each state? How should representatives be chosen?

6. Should the size and / or population of the states be a factor in making decisions? Why or why not?

7. What powers should the states have? Why?

8. How should problems between the states be solved? Why?

9. Anything else?

Our Government Plan

Powers of the Federal Government:

Powers of the states:

Leader and powers:

Making Laws:

Representing the people:

Other:

Put It in Writing

Objective: The student will be able to describe the basic structure of the U.S. Constitution.

Materials:

Making Plans (Springboard handout)
U.S. Constitution (online, in a textbook, etc.)
Main Points of the U.S. Constitution (2-page handout)

Terms to know:

document - important writing, as for a government
ratify - approve, as a document or law

Procedure:

- After reviewing the Springboard, remind the student(s) that *the Constitution is the plan describing how the U.S. government works*. Then go on to explain that *in this lesson the student(s) will look at that famous document to learn "the basics" of it*.

- Distribute a copy of the Constitution and the "Main Points of the U.S. Constitution" handout. Explain that *this is a kind of Constitution scavenger hunt and does NOT require careful reading of the Constitution or a complete understanding of its words. The purpose is for the student(s) to get a BASIC understanding of the way the Constitution is organized and learn some of its main ideas*. (**NOTE:** Individual sections of the document are examined in more detail in future lessons.) Depending upon student ability, the outline can be completed as a teacher-directed activity, or student(s) can examine the Constitution and fill in the outline details individually or in pairs.

- Have the student(s) share / review their ideas and discuss the following:
  - ? In general, how is the Constitution organized? (*It includes an introduction, a body, and amendments. Each branch of government is described in a section with clauses providing details for each, etc.*)
  - ? Why is it helpful to understand how the document is organized? (*It allows it to be read easier; information and details to be more easily located, etc.*)

©InspirEd Educators, Inc.

Making Plans

What would be the MAIN reasons why people make plans? _____

_____

_____

_____

What main details would need to be included in plans? _____

_____

_____

_____

Why SHOULD we make plans? _____

_____

_____

_____

Why is it helpful to write down our plans? _____

_____

_____

_____

What happens if plans change? What do we do then? _____

_____

_____

_____

A constitution is a plan for how a government will work. Why do you think
it is it important that it be written and shared with "the people?" _____

_____

_____

_____

_____

Main Points of the U.S. Constitution

I. INTRODUCTION

   A. The introduction is called the _____.

   B. It states WHY the Constitution was written.

II. BODY

   A. Article I

   1. Section 1 refers to the _____ Branch of government.

      a. This legislature includes the _____

      b. And the _____

   2. Section 2 refers to the House of Representatives

      a. Representatives are elected every _____ years.

      b. Representatives must be at least _____ years old.

      c. Representatives must live in the _____ they represent.

      d. House of Representative numbers are based on _____.

      e. The leader of the House is called the Speaker of the House.

   3. Section 3 refers to the Senate

      a. Senators serve for _____.

      b. Senators must be at least _____ years old.

      c. Senators must live in the state they will represent.

      d. The President of the Senate is the _____.

   4. Section 4 says Congress must meet _____.

   5. Section 5 says a "quorum," a certain number of members, must be present to do anything.

   6. Section 6 says that Members will receive pay for this job.

   7. Section 7 describes how a _____.

   8. Section 8 describes 18 specific powers of Congress such as (List 3 main powers.):

      a. _____

      b. _____

      c. _____

   9. Section 9 describes 8 limits placed on Congress (List 2 main limits to its powers.):

      a. _____

      b. _____

10. Section 10 says there are also things the states cannot do such as (List 2 main powers the states do not have.):

     a. _____

     b. _____

B. Article II

  1. Section 1 creates the office of the _____.

    a. The President must be at least _____ years old.

    b. He/She must be born in the United States

  2. Section 2 names the powers of the President (Name 2 main powers.):

     a. _____

     b. _____

  3. Section 3 says the President shall give a state of the union speech

  4. Section 4 explains why the President might be _____.

C. _____

  1. Section 1 creates the _____.

  2. Section 2 describes the types of cases that can be heard

  3. Section 3 explains the crime of _____.

D. Article IV

  1. Section 1 says that states must honor the laws of others.

  2. Section 2 ensures citizens of one state are treated equally in others.

  3. Section 3 explains how _____ the Union.

  4. Section 4 ensures fair treatment of states by the federal government.

E. Article V

  1. This article explains how to _____ the Constitution.

  2. Amendments must then be ratified by _____ of the states.

F. Article VI

  1. This article explains the role of the Constitution.

  2. It also says U.S. officers must take _____.

G. Article VII

  1. This article notes that nine states must ratify the Constitution.

  2. It also lists _____.

III. AMENDMENTS

A. The first ten amendments are called _____.

B. The rest of the amendments are changes made or things added to the Constitution since it was ratified.

I. INTRODUCTION

A. The introduction is called the _____*Preamble*_____.

B. It states WHY the Constitution was written.

II. BODY

A. Article I

1. Section 1 refers to the _____*Legislative*_____ Branch of government.

   a. This legislature includes the _____*Senate*_____

   b. And the _____***House of Representatives***_____

2. Section 2 refers to the House of Representatives

   a. Representatives are elected every _____*two*_____ years.

   b. Representatives must be at least _____*25*_____ years old.

   c. Representatives must live in the _____*state*_____ they represent.

   d. House of Representative numbers are based on ***states' populations***.

   e. The leader of the House is called the Speaker of the House.

3. Section 3 refers to the Senate

   a. Senators serve for _____***6 years; 6-year terms***_____.

   b. Senators must be at least _____*30*_____ years old.

   c. Senators must live in the state they will represent.

   d. The President of the Senate is the _____*vice president*_____.

4. Section 4 says Congress must meet _____***at least once per year***_____.

5. Section 5 says a "quorum," a certain number of members, must be present to do anything.

6. Section 6 says that Members will receive pay for this job.

7. Section 7 describes how a _____***bill becomes a law; law is made***_____.

8. Section 8 describes 18 specific powers of Congress such as (List 3 main powers.):

   a-c. ***Answers will vary and could include: establish the army and navy, establish post offices, create courts, regulate trade between the states, declare war, raise money, etc.***

9. Section 9 describes 8 limits placed on Congress (List 2 main limits to its powers.):

   a-b. ***Answers will vary and could include: cannot suspend habeas corpus (protection from unfair imprisonment), bill of attainder (legislature naming criminals without trials), etc; cannot pass laws that favor one state over another, cannot take money without a law, cannot give titles (duke, count, earl, etc. - like the king could), etc.***

10. Section 10 says there are also things the states cannot do such as (List 2 main powers the states do not have.):

   a-b. *Answers will vary but could include: to make their own money, declare war, tax goods from other states, have a navy, etc.*

B. Article II

  1. Section 1 creates the office of the _____ *president* _____.

    a. The President must be at least _____ *35* _____ years old.

    b. He/She must be born in the United States

  2. Section 2 names the powers of the President (Name 2 main powers.):

    a-b. *Answers will vary but could include: serves as commander in chief of the armed forces, can pardon criminals, can have a cabinet to serve as aides, can make treaties, pick judges and other members of government, etc.*

  3. Section 3 says the President shall give a state of the union speech

  4. Section 4 explains why the President might be _____ *impeached and/or removed from office* _____.

C. _____ *Article III* _____

  1. Section 1 creates the _____ *Supreme Court* _____.

  2. Section 2 describes the types of cases that can be heard

  3. Section 3 explains the crime of _____ *treason* _____.

D. Article IV

  1. Section 1 says that states must honor the laws of others.

  2. Section 2 ensures citizens of one state are treated equally in others.

  3. Section 3 explains how _____ *new states enter* _____ the Union.

  4. Section 4 ensures fair treatment of states by the federal government.

E. Article V

  1. This article explains how to _____ *amend* _____ the Constitution.

  2. Amendments must then be ratified by _____ *3/4* _____ of the states.

F. Article VI

  1. This article explains the role of the Constitution.

  2. It also says U.S. officers must take _____ *an oath of office* _____.

G. Article VII

  1. This article notes that nine states must ratify the Constitution.

  2. It also lists _____ *the signers* _____.

III. AMENDMENTS

A. The first ten amendments are called _____ *The Bill of Rights* _____.

B. The rest of the amendments are changes made or things added to the Constitution since it was ratified.

Springboard:
Students should complete the "Making a Statement" handout.
(*The king, the people, the "I," and the state. Explanations may vary.*)

Objective: The student will be able to explain how the Preamble of the U.S. Constitution outlines what our government does.

Materials:	Making a Statement (Springboard handout) Pieces of the Preamble (handout) What Does the Government Do? (cut out cards)
Terms to know:	**popular sovereignty** - the idea that the government answers to the people **preamble** - opening statement of a document **citizen** - member of a state or nation

Procedure:

- After reviewing the Springboard, introduce the term "popular sovereignty" and ask the student(s) which of these statements reflects that *(# 2 and arguably 4)*. Explain that "We the people" is the opening statement of the Constitution's preamble (review term). The preamble is important because it is really a statement of what our government intends to do.

- Distribute "Pieces of the Preamble" and have student(s) work individually, in pairs or small groups to complete the handout.

- Have them share their answers (*in order : 4, 6, 1, 7, 5, 2, 3.*) remind the student(s) that *the Preamble introduces the Constitution and explains why the Constitution was written*.

- Then group students into pairs (**individual students** should work with parent/teacher), giving each a set of "What Does the Government Do?" cards. Using their "Pieces of the Preamble" handout as a guide, have the student(s) sort the cards into categories based on what the Constitution was written to accomplish.

- Have the pairs share their groupings and discuss. (*Answers may vary, but should be explained.*)

Making A Statement

DIRECTIONS: Read the four statements and answer the questions below.

> 1. *"By order of the king...."*
>
> 2. *"We the people...."*
>
> 3. *"I hereby demand ...."*
>
> 4. *"The state of Florida passed a law..."*

? Tell who holds power in each of statement. Then tell how you know.

1. _____

_____

_____

2. _____

_____

_____

3. _____

_____

_____

4. _____

_____

_____

? Which statement do you think would **MOST** make people do as they are "told"? Why? _____

_____

_____

_____

_____

Pieces of the Preamble

DIRECTIONS: The Preamble of the U.S. Constitution states what our government is going to do. Read each statement and write the numbers from the "Phase Bank" where they fit. Then tell why YOU THINK each is important.

_____ We the people of the United States, in order to form a more perfect Union,

_____ Establish justice,

_____ insure domestic tranquility,

_____ provide for the common defense,

_____ promote the general welfare and,

_____ secure the Blessings of Liberty to ourselves and our Posterity (future),

_____ do ordain and establish this Constitution for the United States of America.

Phrase Bank:

1. The government should make sure people live in peace.

2. The government should protect our freedoms.

3. The plan for government will be written to do all of these things.

4. The government and the people should work together.

5. The government should help people have better lives.

6. The government should be fair for everyone.

7. The government should make sure the people are safe.

©InspirEd Educators, Inc.

WHAT DOES THE GOVERNMENT DO?

People in the U.S. elect leaders to represent them in government.	Every state in the Union is represented in the federal government.	We have a number of national holidays that Americans celebrate.
Citizens of the United States can vote no matter what race or gender they are.	A citizen cannot be put on trial for a crime without a lawyer to help them.	The United States government outlawed slavery in 1865.
The government pays for police and firefighters.	The government makes sure we have clean air and water.	The government watches out to make sure people do not enter the country illegally.
The government pays for doctors and medicine for the elderly and poor.	There are many museums and libraries paid for by the government.	All children in the United States can go to school for free.
Citizens can freely complain about their government in the United States.	There are many government programs to help kids pay for college.	The government passes laws that make it a crime to destroy another's property.
The government pays for an army, navy, air force and marine force.	The government provides food for poor families.	The government owns many parks and other nature areas.
The government sends soldiers to other countries.	Cars have to pass inspections to make sure they are safe to drive.	The government puts people in prison who have committed crimes.
Everyone's vote counts the same in the United States.	The government provides houses for those that cannot afford them.	Food and medicine must be approved for safety by the government.
The government prints all the money used in the United States.	The government builds bridges, highways and roads.	The government collects taxes from the citizens.
The government makes sure people are hired and fired fairly.	The government pays for research to cure diseases.	The government passes laws to makes sure that workers are safe.
The government oversees safety on airplanes.	Elections in the United States are fair and free.	The government delivers mail for every state in the Union.

Laying Down the Law

Objective: The student will be able to explain the main job of the legislative branch.

Materials: What Does Congress Do? (Springboard handout)
            Solving Problems (handout)
            Write Your Own Bill (handout)
            Sample Bill (handout or transparency)

Terms to know: bill - written plan for a new law

Procedure:

- During discussion of the Springboard, review the structure of the legislative branch basics from the Constitution lesson. *(Congress has two houses: the Senate with 100 members - 2 per state and the House of Representatives with 435 members elected from their states based on population.)* Explain that <u>while Congress has many responsibilities, its main job is lawmaking.</u>

- (**NOTE:** Depending on student ability this simulation may take more than one day, so plan accordingly.) Distribute "Solving Problems" and explain that <u>most of the laws Congress enacts are written to address problems</u>. Allow a few minutes for the student(s) to answer the questions and briefly share ideas. (Use their ideas to group.)

- **For group instruction** organize students into "committees" based on similar problem interests from the "Solving Problems" handout (or assign). Distribute the "Write Your Own Bill" handout and review the writing process using the sample provided. Then allow ample time for groups to write their own bills.

- When completed, organize the committees into two large groups (the House and Senate, with the House group about 4x the size of the Senate) and briefly discuss what makes a "good" law. *(Laws must be fair, easy to enforce or put into action, be clear and easy to understand, etc.)* Have each committee take turns presenting its bill to its own "house" and vote on each.

- Any that pass (by more than half) should be sent to the other house for a vote there. (If time allows, have the bill's "sponsors" explain them before this vote.)

- **For individualized instruction** the parent/teacher should form a "committee" with the student to write a bill and then discuss how things in it may need to change to get more support in order to pass.

- Complete the lesson by summarizing:
  - <u>*Bills are proposed in one of the houses of Congress and then sent to a committee for review and changes.*</u>
  - <u>*Members present their bills and debate them in both houses.*</u>
  - <u>*To become a law, a bill must pass in its exact form by a majority in BOTH houses of Congress. It can be changed and re-voted upon until it does so.*</u>
  - <u>*If both houses cannot pass a bill, it is "dead" and does not become a law.*</u>
  - <u>*Once the bill passes Congress, it is sent to the president to be ratified or rejected (addressed in next lesson).*</u>

WHAT DOES CONGRESS DO?

Article I: Section 8 of the Constitution:

Clause 1: Congress has the power to set and collect taxes and pay the debts of the United States (including the military and other costs).

Clause 2: To borrow money to pay those bills

Clause 3: To oversee trade with other countries, between states, and with the Indian Tribes;

Clause 4: To control immigration (people coming into the nation)

Clause 5: To print money... and set weights and measures for the country;

Clause 6: To oversee punishment of counterfeiting (making fake money);

Clause 7: To run the Post Office;

Clause 8: To oversee and protect people's rights to inventions and writings;

Clause 9: To hold hearings;

Clause 10: To be in charge of crimes taking place on the high seas (oceans);

Clause 11: To declare War;

Clause 12: To organize and pay for Armies...

Clause 13: To organize and pay for a Navy;

Clause 14: To make the rules for the government and the military;

Clause 15: To pay for the Militia (soldiers, etc.) to carry out the Laws of the Union...

Clause 16: To organize and arm the Militia ...

Clause 17: To be in charge of all lands owned by the federal government;

Clause 18: To make all federal laws.

Name and explain 3 ways Congress (the legislative branch) affects your life:

1. _____

_____

_____

_____

2. _____

_____

_____

_____

3. _____

_____

_____

_____

Solving Problems

Make a list of problems that America faces. List big problems and small, nearby or far away -- anything you can think of! _____

_____

_____

_____

_____

_____

_____

_____

_____

Look over your list and find some problems that have things in common (traffic problems, housing, money, etc.). List any MAIN problem groups you can find:

_____

_____

_____

List your ideas about how to solve one or more of these problems in a big or small way. List anything you can think of! _____

_____

_____

_____

Then choose one or two main problems you think the government might be able to solve or help solve. Explain how. _____

_____

_____

_____

Write Your Own Bill

U.S. House of Representatives / U.S. Senate

Bill # _____

Introduced By: _____

Title:

Problem Statement:

Plan for Action:

Idea Explained:

Planned Results:

Time until Law Takes Effect:

SAMPLE BILL

U.S. House of Representatives / U.S. Senate
Bill # *S-101*

Introduced By: *(Students names)*

Title: *A bill to provide free babysitting to families that earn less than $30,000 per year.*

Problem Statement:

There are many families in our community that are poor. Babysitting is very costly. Many families can get work, but by the time they pay a babysitter, they do not have enough money to pay for food, rent, clothes, doctors, and other needs.

Plan for Action:

Families that prove they earn less than $30,000 per year will be given a coupon to use for any child care center or babysitter. The coupon can be used to pay the cost of child care. The center or babysitter then sends in the coupon to be paid by the government.

Idea Explained:

Families that cannot afford child care have a very hard time making their lives better. Even if they can find work, they often do not make enough to meet their needs. Many people remain poor for this reason.

Planned Results:

This bill will mean needy families can earn money from working. They can pay for their needs and save for the future. They may be able to live in better homes, and maybe pay for school to get better jobs. In the end they will not be as poor. Meanwhile, babysitters will get paid and children will be cared for while their parents work.

Time until Law Takes Effect:

This law can take effect as soon as it is passed and people can be told about it.

©InspirEd Educators, Inc.

Hail to the Chief

Objective: The student will be able to describe the main duties and powers of the President of the United States.

Materials: Qualification Questions (Springboard handout)
Leading the Nation (handout)
A President's Day (handout)

Terms to know: **qualification** - skill, education, or other factor a person must have for a job
pardon - to forgive for a crime
treaty - agreement between two or more countries
execute - put into action
veto - say "no" to a law

Procedure:

- After reviewing the Springboard, explain that *in this lesson the student(s) will learn about the job of the president.*

- Distribute copies of "Leading the Nation" and explain that *the president does many things, some (the first seven items on the chart) are POWERS of the president stated in the Constitution, and others (the last four) are DUTIES that over time have become part of the president's job.* Have the student(s) work individually, in pairs, or small groups to study the chart and make their ratings.

- Have them share their ideas and discuss. *(Ratings may vary but should be justified and spark discussion.)*

- Then hand out "A President's Day." Explain that *now that the student(s) have an idea of what the president does, they should create what they think a typical day might be like.* Have the student(s) work individually, in pairs or small groups to make up their schedules.

- Have them share their schedules and discuss the following. (*Answers will vary but should be justified and spark discussion*):
  - ? Which responsibilities of the president do you think take up the MOST time? Why?
  - ? What other things do you think the president might or should do other than what you learned in the lesson?
  - ? What do you think is the MOST IMPORTANT job of the president? Why?
  - ? Based on what you've learned, what other qualifications or personality traits do you think a president should have?

QUALIFICATION QUESTIONS

DIRECTIONS: Read the qualifications and other rules for being the President of the United States. Tell why you think the founding fathers may have put each into the Constitution.

The president must be at least thirty-five years old. _____

_____

_____

_____

_____

_____

The president must be born in the United States. _____

_____

_____

_____

_____

_____

The president can only serve two 4-year terms in office. _____

_____

_____

_____

_____

_____

The president cannot earn any money other than his pay while in office. _____

_____

_____

_____

_____

_____

©InspirEd Educators, Inc.

LEADING THE NATION

DIRECTIONS: Read about the powers and duties of the United States president. Rate how important you think each is from 1 (least important) to 10 (most important) and explain your ideas.

Power, Duty, or Role	Example	Rating	Explain
Serves as commander-in-chief of the army, navy, and other armed forces	Sends troops to an African country to keep order		
Can pardon someone for a federal crime	Pardons the crime of a aide who was found guilty of tax crimes		
Can make treaties with other countries	Signs a new trade agreement with Mexico		
Can name people to important jobs in the government	Chooses a new Supreme Court justice when one retires		
Must execute (put into action) the laws of the United States	In charge of the federal lawyers who try a man for a terror plot		
Can give Executive Orders	Signs an order to protect fish on the Pacific coast		
Can ratify or veto bills passed by Congress	Signs a bill into law making it a crime to carry guns in hospitals		
Serves as the "face" of the United States all over the world	Attends a ceremony in honor of a Russian poet		
Is the leader of his/her political party	Gives a speech to help a woman in Texas get elected to Congress		
Meets with leaders of other countries	Hosts a state dinner for the German president		
Can ask Congress to pass laws	Urges Congress to pass tougher laws on crime		

A President's Day

DIRECTIONS: The president has a LOT to do! Make up a schedule to show what you think a day in the life of the President of the United States might be like.

7:00 AM

8:00 AM

9:00 AM

10:00 AM

11:00 AM

12:00 PM

1:00 PM

2:00 PM

3:00 PM

4:00 PM

5:00 PM

6:00 PM

Evening

Springboard:
Students should study the "United States Court System" diagram and answer the questions.

Objective: The student will be able to describe how cases come to the Supreme Court and the importance of judicial review.

Materials:
The United States Court System (Springboard handout)
You Do the Review (handout)

Terms to know:
court - a judge or judges that hear the facts of a case and make decisions
appeal - to ask for another ruling
violate - break a law
judicial review - the right of the Supreme Court to look at lower court rulings to see if they violate the Constitution
justices - members of the Supreme Court

Procedure:
- While reviewing the Springboard, make sure that student(s) understand why there are so many levels of courts. Review the term "judicial review" and explain that _while there are many courts in the U.S., the Supreme Court is the highest court in the land so it has the last word in any case it hears. The MAIN job of the Supreme Court is to REVIEW laws and cases to ensure that they do not violate the U.S. Constitution in any way_. Go on to explain that _in this lesson the student(s) will examine some real Supreme Court cases to learn what the Court does_.
- Distribute "You Do the Review" and review the directions. Have student(s) work individually, in pairs, or small groups as "justices" to read each case and record their opinions and justifications.
- Have the student(s) share / compare their ideas. (**For individualized instruction** or if student opinions seem too similar, play "devil's advocate" and argue the other side of each case.) Note that _there are often different opinions among Supreme Court justices so in cases so when that happens, the Court's decision is the view held by more than half of them_.
- Reveal to student(s) that in every one of these cases, the Supreme Court disagreed with the lower courts. Discuss what student(s) think of these decisions and the important outcomes of judicial review:
  - **Brown:** The court determined that separate schools cannot be equal, because they are separate.
  - **Gideon:** The Court said that he could not have a fair trial without a lawyer.
  - **Hazelwood:** The Court ruled that the principal did not violate free speech as long as he had reasonable concerns about the school environment

THE UNITED STATES COURT SYSTEM

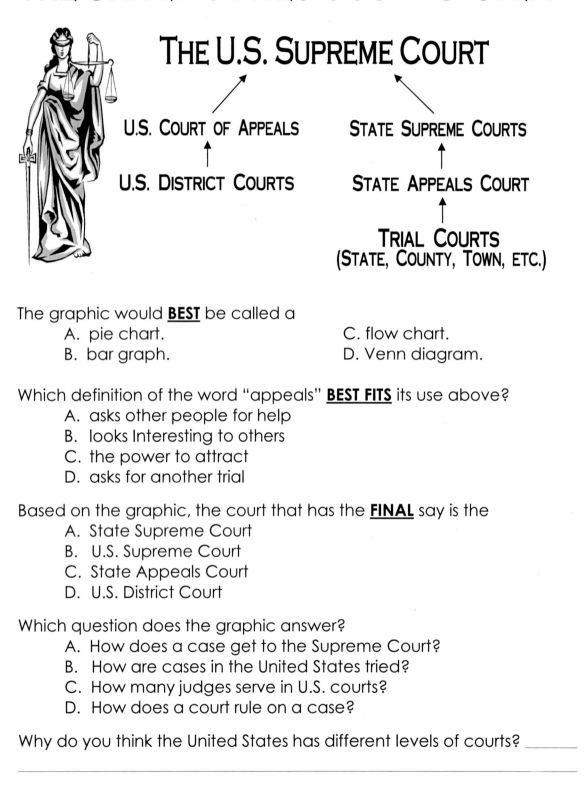

THE U.S. SUPREME COURT

U.S. COURT OF APPEALS   STATE SUPREME COURTS

U.S. DISTRICT COURTS   STATE APPEALS COURT

TRIAL COURTS
(STATE, COUNTY, TOWN, ETC.)

The graphic would **BEST** be called a
    A. pie chart.   C. flow chart.
    B. bar graph.   D. Venn diagram.

Which definition of the word "appeals" **BEST FITS** its use above?
    A. asks other people for help
    B. looks Interesting to others
    C. the power to attract
    D. asks for another trial

Based on the graphic, the court that has the **FINAL** say is the
    A. State Supreme Court
    B. U.S. Supreme Court
    C. State Appeals Court
    D. U.S. District Court

Which question does the graphic answer?
    A. How does a case get to the Supreme Court?
    B. How are cases in the United States tried?
    C. How many judges serve in U.S. courts?
    D. How does a court rule on a case?

Why do you think the United States has different levels of courts? _____

_____

_____

_____

_____

THE U.S. SUPREME COURT

U.S. COURT OF APPEALS   STATE SUPREME COURTS

U.S. DISTRICT COURTS   STATE APPEALS COURT

TRIAL COURTS
(STATE, COUNTY, TOWN, ETC.)

The graphic would **BEST** be called a

A. pie chart.

B. bar graph.

C. flow chart. *

D. Venn diagram.

(The chart doesn't look like a pie or have bars, but the "flow" of information shown by arrows offers a big hint to the answer.)

Which definition of the word "appeals" **BEST FITS** its use above?

A. asks other people for help

B. looks Interesting to others

C. the power to attract

D. asks for another trial *

(By substituting each choice for the term in the graphic, Choice D is the only one that makes sense. Students will likely recognize a link between trials and courts.)

Based on the graphic, the court that has the **FINAL** say is the

A. State Supreme Court

B. U.S. Supreme Court *

C. State Appeals Court

D. U.S. District Court

(The U.S. Supreme Court is at the top of the graphic; everything else flows upward, higher to it.)

Which question does the graphic answer?

A. How does a case get to the Supreme Court? *

B. How are cases in the United States tried?

C. How many judges serve in U.S. courts?

D. How does a court rule on a case?

(There is not enough information given to determine B, C, or D. The chart shows how cases move through the courts to get to the Supreme Court.)

Why do you think the United States has different levels of courts?: *Answers will vary, but note that <u>the court system allows cases to be reviewed several times</u>. Judges and juries can make mistakes, or new evidence can turn up over time. So those convicted can "appeal" to higher courts to have their cases reviewed or retried.*

YOU DO THE REVIEW

Your Face Here

DIRECTIONS: As a "Supreme Court justice," review each case and explain if and why you agree or disagree with each lower court's ruling.

Brown vs. Board of Education (1954): A law in Kansas said schools could divide students based on race. Topeka, Kansas had separate schools for black and white students. Linda Brown, a young African American girl, had to walk very far to her school. She was not allowed to go to a closer school which was only for white students. She claimed her rights promised by the U.S. Constitution were violated. A federal district court said the law was fine. The court ruled that students could go to separate schools as long as their schools were "equal." _____

_____

_____

_____

Gideon vs. Wainwright (1963): Clarence Gideon was charged with breaking into a bar and stealing money and other things. He was poor and could not afford to pay a lawyer. He claimed the Constitution says "all citizens have the right to a lawyer." But the judge in the case would not pay for one, since the crime was too minor and not worth the cost. So Gideon was found guilty and sent to prison for five years. _____

_____

_____

_____

Hazelwood vs. Kuhlmeier (1988): The principal at Hazelwood East High School took two pages out of the school paper before it was printed. He said two students' articles were not things that should be in a school paper. The students took the school district to court. They said the principal violated their right to free speech. The U.S. Court of Appeals agreed with the students. The court ruled that a school paper is not a classroom. Students have the right to free speech as long as they don't hurt others or keep them from learning.

_____

_____

_____

_____

Balancing Act

Springboard:
>   Students should complete the "Working Together" handout.

Objective: The student will be able to explain how the system of checks and balances work.

Materials:	Working Together (Springboard handout)
	Executive, Legislative, and Judicial Power Cards (cut out cards)
	The Balance of Power (handout)
Terms to know:	**checks and balances** - system that separates powers among branches and assigns powers that can stop another branch to keep any of the three from becoming too powerful
	summary - statement of the main ideas of a reading
	military - army, navy, air force, etc.
	impeach - charge and try for crimes in office

Procedure:

· After discussing the Springboard, explain that _although the three branches of the government work together, they each have different powers. The founding fathers set up the system of checks and balances (review term) so no one branch would become too powerful_. Go on to explain that _in this lesson the student(s) will play a game to learn how checks and balances work._

· **For group instruction** students should play the game in groups of threes. **For individualized instruction** the student and parent/teacher should play with a third player, if at all possible (or one player can play two roles). Before beginning the game, decide which player will represent each branch of government.

· Distribute one set of "Power Cards" (20 per student) to the players representing each branch: Executive, Legislative, and Judicial. (**NOTE:** Some cards are duplicated since they can be used in several instances.) Depending on student background and ability, review the card meanings before playing.

· To begin the game, one player places one of his/her cards in the center of the group, reading it aloud. The other two should study their cards to see if they have a power that could check or balance it, announce the power, explain how it serves as a check or balance, and lay it on the "power" it refers to. (_Answers may vary, but are acceptable if reasonable and explained. In cases of disagreement, the teacher should serve as the "judge."_)

· Players should take turns until all cards are used or no more can be.

· Have student(s) complete "The Balance of Power" individually or in playing groups.

· Have them share their answers and discuss, using the "Balance of Power" analysis questions as a guide. (_Answers may vary, if well-reasoned, and should spark discussion._)

WORKING TOGETHER

DIRECTIONS: For each statement, tell if it is a role of the legislative, executive, or judicial branch. Underline the words that provide clues for your answers.

_____ Programs are set up to help people get recycling bins.

_____ People are given tickets if they don't recycle.

_____ A law is passed that makes it a crime not to recycle.

_____ Police check houses for recycling bins.

_____ Recycling centers are opened to make recycling easy.

_____ A law requires cans, papers, and plastic be recycled.

_____ People are put on trial if they do not pay their tickets.

_____ A committee is formed to decide if a law is needed.

_____ Judges decide how to punish people who don't recycle.

Now, write a short summary of what each branch of government does:

Legislative - _____

_____

_____

_____

Executive - _____

_____

_____

_____

Judicial - _____

_____

_____

_____

Why is it important for the three branches to work together? _____

_____

_____

_____

_____

WORKING TOGETHER
SUGGESTIONS FOR ANSWERS

DIRECTIONS: For each statement, tell if it is a role of the legislative, executive, or judicial branch. Underline the words that provide clues for your answers.

Executive   Programs are <u>set up</u> to help people get recycling bins.

Executive   People are <u>given tickets</u> if they fail to recycle.

Legislative   A <u>law is passed</u> that makes it a crime not to recycle.

Executive   <u>Police check</u> houses for recycling bins.

Executive   Recycling <u>centers are opened</u> to make recycling easy.

Legislative   <u>A law requires </u>cans, papers, and plastic be recycled.

Judicial   People are <u>put on trial</u> if they do not pay their tickets.

Legislative   A <u>committee is formed</u> to decide if a law is needed.

Judicial   <u>Judges decide</u> how to punish people who don't recycle.

Now, write a short summary of what each branch of government does:

Legislative - *Answers may vary, but students should understand that the MAIN job of the legislative branch is to decide what laws are needed and pass them.*

Executive - *Answers may vary, but students should understand that the MAIN job of the executive branch is to carry out the laws and plans of the legislative branch. Basically, the executive branch puts the laws into "action."*

Judicial - *Answers may vary, but students should understand that the MAIN job of the judicial branch is to decide if laws have been broken and what to do if it has been. It also holds the power of judicial review.*

Why is it important for the three branches to work together?
Answers may vary, but each branch has its own powers, which interact and support the powers of the other two branches. A law is of little value if it is not carried out or if people are not punished for disobeying it!

EXECUTIVE POWER CARDS

Appoints Supreme Court and other federal judges.

Can veto laws passed by Congress.

Can make treaties with other countries.

Appoints Supreme Court and other federal judges.

The vice president votes to break ties in the Senate.

The president can pardon people for their crimes.

The president can call Congress into session.

The president is the commander-in-chief of the military.

The president appoints all generals (high leaders) in the army.

Can issue executive orders.

The president puts laws into action.

The president puts laws into action.

The president puts laws into action.

The president can set aside (or commute) punishments of criminals.

The president can create offices to see that laws are carried out.

The president can hire and fire people in the executive branch.

The president can directly appeal to the people.

The president can only serve two four year terms.

The president can suggest laws to be passed.

The president chooses people to speak for the U.S. abroad.

LEGISLATIVE POWER CARDS

 Congress makes all the laws.	 Congress makes all the laws.	 Congress makes all the laws.	 Holds hearings and must approve Supreme Court judges.	 Congress can declare war.
 Congress sets aside money to pay for the military.	 Congress decides what taxes people must pay.	 Congress is in charge of all federal lands and buildings.	 The Senate must approve all high-level army officers.	 Congress decides which areas federal courts serve.
 Congress approves treaties.	 Can hold hearings about misdeeds of judges.	 Congress must approve people the president appoints.	 The Senate can impeach the president or others.	 Congress decides how tax money is spent.
 Congress can make new courts.	 Senators can serve an unlimited number of six-year terms.	 Members of the House of Representatives serve two-year terms.	 The House decides on charges to impeach president.	 Can pass laws vetoed by the president if 2/3 members vote to do so.

JUDICIAL POWER CARDS

This branch decides if laws violate the Constitution.

This branch decides if laws violate the Constitution.

This branch decides if laws violate the Constitution.

This branch decides if laws violate the Constitution.

This branch decides if laws violate the Constitution.

This branch decides if laws violate the Constitution.

This branch decides if laws violate the Constitution.

This branch decides if laws violate the Constitution.

This branch decides if laws violate the Constitution.

This branch decides if laws violate the Constitution.

Special tax courts hear cases about tax laws.

Supreme Court cases are decided by at least 5 of 9 justices.

The Constitution cannot be violated!

Justices cannot be removed without VERY good cause.

The Supreme Court's Chief Justice leads Senate hearings to impeach.

The Supreme Court has the final say on all matters of law.

Special courts hear cases about the military.

Supreme Court judges serve for life (or until they retire).

The Supreme Court decides if it will hear cases from lower courts.

Supreme Court rulings can only be changed by the Court.

The Balance of Power

Who do you think won the game? Why?

Which, if any, branch of the U.S. government has more power than the others? Explain your answer.

Which powers were not checked by another branch in the game? Do you think all powers SHOULD be checked? Explain.

Based on the game, which branch do you think has its power checked the MOST? Why? Which branch do you think has its power checked the LEAST? Why?

Why do you think the founding fathers set up checks and balances in the U.S. government?

Is it a good idea to have three government branches? Why?

Do you think a government needs checks and balances? Why or why not?

| **Springboard:** |
| Students should complete the "I Know My Rights!" brainstorm. |
| *(Answers will vary.)* |

Objective: The student will be able to describe rights granted in the Bill of Rights.

Materials: I Know My Rights! (Springboard handout)
The Bill of Rights (handout)
What's It Worth to YOU? (handout)

Terms to know: **amendments** - changes to a document
trial - hearing to decide court cases
jury - group of people that watch a trial and vote on the ruling (usually guilty or not)
witness - someone who tells what they know of events
due process - the right to justice and fair treatment under the law

Procedure:

· While reviewing the Springboard, make a list on the board or other display of the student(s) ideas about rights. Explain that *after the Constitution was written, several states were not satisfied with the final product. They would not ratify the document unless the rights of citizens were specifically stated, so the first ten amendments (see term), known as the Bill of Rights, were added before the Constitution could go into effect*.

· Distribute "The Bill of Rights" (simplified for student comprehension) and "What's It Worth to YOU?" Have the student(s) work individually, in pairs, or small groups to read the Bill of Rights and chose those they consider most important.

· Have the student(s) share and compare their ideas. Then revisit the Springboard list to see how many of the rights named are included in the Bill of Rights, and discuss the following questions

  ? Which rights(s) guarantee "personal" freedoms? How are these different from the other Amendments? (*Amendments I-IV are personal freedoms; these rights apply to EVERYONE in the United States.*)

  ? Which right(s) do you think are considered "due process" (review term) for those charged with crimes? How are these amendments different from the others? How do these guarantee "due process?" (*Amendments V-VIII apply to people accused of crimes. These provide basic protections to ensure fair treatment under the law.*)

  ? Which amendment guarantees the rights of states? (*Amendment X gives any powers NOT stated as being those of the federal government to the states. This means that if the Constitution doesn't say otherwise, the states can decide on issues such as whether or not people found guilty of murder can be put to death.*)

I Know My Rights!

I HAVE RIGHTS!!

DIRECTIONS: List all the rights you can think of that you and other citizens of the United States have. Include things we have the "right NOT to do," also. Fill in as many blanks as you can!

_____   _____
_____   _____
_____   _____
_____   _____
_____   _____
_____   _____
_____   _____
_____   _____
_____   _____
_____   _____
_____   _____
_____   _____
_____   _____
_____   _____
_____   _____
_____   _____
_____   _____
_____   _____
_____   _____
_____   _____
_____   _____
_____   _____

THE BILL OF RIGHTS

Amendment I
Congress cannot make any laws about religion or stop anyone from the practice of their religion. They cannot make laws that limit freedom of speech. There can be no laws stopping people or the press (reporters, newspapers, etc.) from saying or writing what they want. No laws can be written to keep people from meeting or speaking out against the government or asking it to make changes.

Amendment II
Congress cannot stop people from having weapons to protect themselves.

Amendment III
People cannot be forced to have soldiers stay in their homes.

Amendment IV
No one can search a person's body, home, or things unless a judge rules that there is a good reason to think a crime has taken place.

Amendment V
No one can be put on trial for a crime unless a court decides there is good reason. No one can be tried for the same crime twice. A person does not have to say anything at his/her trial. The government cannot punish people without a trial and their property cannot be taken away unless the government pays for it.

Amendment VI
A person charged with a crime has a right to a speedy trial, and cannot be held in jail without one. The trial must be open so everyone knows what is going on. Those accused have the right to know what they are on trial for. They also must be allowed to see and hear what others say and offer their own witnesses. The accused also has the right to a lawyer to help at their trial.

Amendment VII
People in civil cases (when two people disagree; not trials for crimes) also have the right to a jury trial.

Amendment VIII
The government cannot make people pay more for bail or fines than is fair for a crime. If found guilty, the punishment cannot be overly cruel (like torture).

Amendment IX
People have other rights that may not be stated in the Constitution.

Amendment X
Any powers not given to Congress should be left to the states or the people.

What's It Worth to YOU?

DIRECTIONS: Study the Bill of Rights and decide which you think are your FIVE MOST IMPORTANT rights. List them, describe the main right(s), and explain your choices.

1. Amendment# _____ Right(s): _____

   Explain: _____

   _____

   _____

   _____

2. Amendment# _____ Right(s): _____

   Explain: _____

   _____

   _____

   _____

3. Amendment# _____ Right(s): _____

   Explain: _____

   _____

   _____

   _____

4. Amendment# _____ Right(s): _____

   Explain: _____

   _____

   _____

   _____

5. Amendment# _____ Right(s): _____

   Explain: _____

   _____

   _____

   _____

Oops!

Springboard:
Students should complete the "Article V of the Constitution" handout.
(Amendments can be 1. proposed by Congress with 2/3rds vote in both houses and ratified by 3/4ths of the state legislatures; 2. proposed by Congress with a 2/3rds vote in both houses and ratified by 3/4ths of state conventions; 3. proposed at a national convention of 2/3ʳᵈ of the states and ratified by 3/4ths of the state legislatures; and 4. proposed at a national convention of 2/3ʳᵈ of the states and ratified by 3/4ths of state conventions. Answers to the last questions may vary.)

Objective: The student will be able to explain the purpose of the Amendment process and describe some notable Amendments to the Constitution.

Materials:　　　　Article V of the Constitution (Springboard handout)
　　　　　　　　　　Change Is Good, Isn't It? (handout)

Procedure:

- (**NOTE:** Depending on ability, it may be necessary to assist some students in completing the Springboard handout.) While discussing answers, explain that *while it is not necessary to be able to explain the exact process for amending the Constitution, it IS important that the document CAN BE amended* and have the student(s) explain why. *(The nation has changed IMMENSELY since the Constitution was written! In 1789 there were fewer than four million Americans living along the eastern coast of the country. Most people were farmers, and the nation was not very powerful in the world. Today there are over 300 million people living all over the 50 states, and the U.S. is the most powerful nation in the world.)*

- **For group instruction** divide students into eight groups, giving each a "Change is Good, Isn't It?" handout. Assign one amendment from the chart to each group. Have each group conduct quick Internet research to learn the background and point of their amendments and create a skit to explain and illustrate or otherwise "teach" the information. **For individualized instruction** the student should research all the amendments to find out the point of each, including examples as appropriate, to fill in the first column of the chart.

- Have the groups perform their skits or share their examples. Those who have not already done so should complete the first column.

- Then they should complete the last column, justifying their ideas.

- Have them share their answers and discuss. (**NOTE:** During the discussion, point out that *fourteen years after the 18ᵗʰ Amendment made alcohol sales illegal, the 21ˢᵗ Amendment was passed to make them legal again*.)

- **EXTENSION:** Have the student(s) read a list of all the amendments and explain why they think the ones included in the lesson were chosen and if others should have been included and why and why or why not. *(Answers will vary and should be explained.)*

　　　　　　　　　　　　　　　　　　©InspirEd Educators, Inc.

Article V of the Constitution

"Congress, whenever two thirds of both Houses think it is necessary, can propose Amendments to this Constitution. This can also be done by the Legislatures of two thirds of the States by calling a national Convention for proposing Amendments. In either Case, amendments will be added when ratified by the Legislatures or Conventions of three fourths of the several States."

What are the four ways amendments can be added to the Constitution?

Proposed by…	Ratified by…

Why do you think the founding fathers added ways to amend the Constitution when they wrote it? _____

_____

_____

_____

_____

Do you think it's important that the document CAN be changed? Why or why not?

_____

_____

_____

_____

_____

Change is Good, Isn't It?

Amendment	What's the Point?	Good Idea? Why or Why Not?
13th		
15th		
16th		
18th		
19th		
22nd		
25th		
26th		

Do the Right Thing

Objective: The student will be able to explain the main things "good citizens" do.

Materials:
And Speaking of Citizens… (Springboard handout)
Getting the Word Out (handout)
art supplies (paper, markers, etc.)

Procedure:

- During discussion of the Springboard, point out that *there are very few things U.S. citizens are FORCED to do (such as obeying the laws). Most acts of citizenship are voluntary and require effort, so there are always some people who participate as citizens (stay informed about government, vote, serve in the armed forces, etc.) and many who don't.* Go on to explain that *in this lesson the student(s) will create pamphlets or posters to persuade everyone to "do the right thing."*

- Distribute "Getting the Word Out" and review the project requirements. The student(s) should choose topics from the list of what "good citizens" do (or topics can be assigned) and work individually, in pairs, or small groups to research their topics as needed and create their pamphlets/posters.

- Have them share their work and discuss the following questions as they apply:
  - ? Which posters/pamphlets do you think were the most persuasive? Why? *(Answers will vary.)*
  - ? How can people be coaxed to vote or participate in other ways when they are not required to do so? *(By appealing to their feelings of duty, guilt, patriotism, etc.)*
  - ? Why do you think voting, volunteering, etc. make us better citizens? How do "good citizens" make the country better? *(Answers may vary and should be explained.)*
  - ? What are some things you can do to be good citizens – as a student and later as an adult? *(Answers may vary but should make sense.)*

And Speaking of Citizens...

A. *"Bad officials are elected by good citizens who do not vote."*
   George Jean Nathan, American journalist

B. *"A job of a citizen is to keep his mouth open."*
   Gunter Grass, German poet and artist

C. *"Citizenship is a tough job that requires the citizen to make his own informed opinion and stand by it"*
   Martha Gellhorn, American journalist

D. *"As citizens, we all (must)... become involved - it's the citizen who changes things."*
   Jose Saramago, Portuguese writer

E. *"Every citizen should be a soldier. This was the case with the Greeks and Romans, and must be that of every free state."*
   Thomas Jefferson, Founding Father and U.S. President

F. *"I'm a very bad citizen. I've never even voted."*
   Jerry Hall, American model and actress

G. *"There is much more to being a ... citizen than reciting the pledge or raising a flag."*
   Jesse Ventura, former pro-wrestler and Minnesota Governor

What are some things "good citizens" do?

Which quote do you MOST agree with, and why?

Which quote do you LEAST agree with, and why?

GETTING THE WORD OUT

Choose one thing that citizens SHOULD do, and make a poster or pamphlet to urge people to do it. Research as needed to find out what citizens in your city, state, etc. need to do and how. When others see your poster/pamphlet, they should WANT to do what they should and know how.

Good citizens:
- Keep up with government and what it does.
- Register and vote in elections.
- Can serve in the armed forces.
- Let others (like people in government) know what you think about a problem.
- Sit on a jury.
- Or any other activity you can think of!

Your project should:
1. Pick your topic and research the details as needed. For example, where do people register to vote? How old to you have to be to join the army? Where do you go? How can a citizen make his/her ideas known? How do you get picked for a jury? Where do you go? Make sure you include any information a "good citizen" would need to know.
2. Explain why this act is important. Why should people do this?
3. Make others want to take action!
4. Make your poster/pamphlet neat and attractive. You want it to get attention so be creative!

- -

SCORING GUIDE

Use this scale to grade your work:

4- Excellent   3 – Good   2- Fair   1 – Poor   0- Unacceptable

	Student	Teacher
Explains importance	_____	_____
Makes people WANT to act	_____	_____
Gives needed information TO act	_____	_____
Neat and creative	_____	_____
Spelling and grammar	_____	_____

GRADE:

COMMENTS:

Springboard:
Students should study the "It's a Party!" information and answer the questions.
(Answers will vary; see definition in Terms to know."

Objective: The student will be able to explain the main role of political parties in the United States.

Materials:

It's a Party! (Springboard handout)
Candidates' Comments (handout)
And Your Comments... (handout)

Terms to know:

political party - group of people with common ideas who work together to get their candidates elected
candidate - one running for office
environment - the world around us
independent - candidate who is not a member of a main party

Procedure:

- After discussion of the Springboard, explain that *the two main political parties in the United States are the Democrats and Republicans, though there are also many smaller parties with less influence*. Go on to explain this lesson *looks at what happens when candidates OTHER THAN Republicans or Democrats run for president*.

- Distribute the "Candidates' Comments" and the "And Your Comments..." handouts. Explain that *the "Candidates' Comments" are from three third-party candidates or independents* (review term) *who have run for president*. The student(s) should read the narratives individually, in pairs, or small groups and complete the "And Now Your Comments" analysis form.

- Have the student(s) share their ideas and discuss. (*Answers will vary but should spark discussion.*)

©InspirEd Educators, Inc.

It's a party!

Members of political parties:

★ Have common ideas about how government should be run.

★ Have common ideas about how the country should be run.

★ Support candidates of the same party.

★ May give their time to support their candidates.

★ Donate money to help their candidates.

★ Try to get voters to vote for their candidate.

How political parties help candidates get elected:

★ Pay for ads on TV, radio, in newspapers, etc.

★ Print, hand out, and display bumper stickers, yard signs, etc.

★ Pay for rallies and other meetings to support their candidates.

★ Make phone calls to get people to donate money and vote.

★ Go door to door to get votes.

★ Spend large amounts of money to help their candidates.

Based on this information, what is a political party? _____

_____

_____

_____

What else do you know about political parties in the United States? _____

_____

_____

_____

Do you think political parties are good or bad for America? Why? _____

_____

_____

_____

Candidates' Comments

Ralph Nader here. I have been very active as a citizen and candidate for a long time. First I worked to force auto makers to produce safer cars. I've also worked to protect the environment. In fact I have run for president four times as a Green Party Candidate. The Green Party's main concern is the environment, so I was a good choice for them.

I also ran twice as an independent, which means no party backed me. I never won many votes in any of those elections, but I did get a lot of attention in 2000! That election was SO close, some people blame me for taking votes from the Democrat, Al Gore, so Republican George W. Bush won. I don't think it mattered, though. People who voted for me may not have even voted at all if I hadn't run. Who knows?

My name is Ross Perot. I am in business and quite good at my work, if my wealth means anything. But in the 1980's I decided to get involved in government in different ways. I was angry with our government for not handling problems it needed to.

Then in 1992 I ran for president. I spent $65 million dollars of my own money to do so! My campaign went well and many people seemed to agree with me on a number of subjects. As a matter of fact, my campaign had the most success of any third-party candidate. I actually won 18% of the vote! I even beat the Republican and Democrat in two states!

In 1996 I started my own party, the Reform Party, and ran again. That time I only got 8% of the vote. I think it was mostly because I was not allowed to appear in the TV debates. Only the Republicans and Democrats had the chance to bring their case before the American people. I say that wasn't fair!

My name is Bob Barr from Georgia. I'm a Republican and have served in Congress for many years. Then in 2008 I ran as another party's candidate for president. You see, I could not support the Republican John McCain. I liked him as a man. I just didn't think he spoke for me and what I believe.

I wanted to give people another choice. So I won the support of the Libertarian Party. Things didn't turn out very well though. I didn't even get 1% of the vote on Election Day. Of course my name wasn't even on the ballot in all states! Third party candidates can only be on the ballot if enough people sign a letter to say that's what they want. My party and I tried, but we couldn't make it in 5 states. I'm sure that hurt my chances. Do you agree?

And Your Comments...

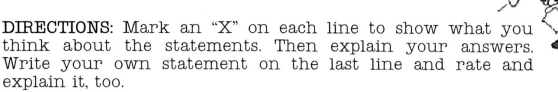

DIRECTIONS: Mark an "X" on each line to show what you think about the statements. Then explain your answers. Write your own statement on the last line and rate and explain it, too.

1. Third party candidates have no chance of winning in the U.S.

Strongly   Strongly
  Agree   Disagree

◄───►

2. Third party candidates receive unfair treatment in the U.S.

Strongly   Strongly
  Agree   Disagree

◄───►

3. Americans need more parties to choose from in the U.S.

Strongly   Strongly
  Agree   Disagree

◄───►

4. _____

Strongly   Strongly
  Agree   Disagree

◄───►

Electing the President

Springboard:
Students should study "The Electoral College."
and answer the questions.

Objective: The student will be able to explain the purpose of the Electoral College.

Materials:

The Electoral College (Springboard handout)
Back in Time (handout)
What's the Point? (handout)

Terms to know:

Electoral College - group that elects the president
elector - person who votes in the Electoral College

Procedure:

- After reviewing the Springboard explain that _in this lesson the student(s) will learn why the Electoral College was established_.
- Distribute "Back in Time." Have the student(s) work individually, in pairs, or small groups to read each scenario and explain how they would have voted as members of the Electoral College <u>BACK THEN</u>.
- Have them share their decisions and justifications and hand out "What's the Point?" The student(s) should complete the analysis questions.
- Again, have the student(s) share their answers and discuss. (_Answers will vary, but the following points should be stressed during discussion_:
  - _The Electoral College was created out of a need to protect the presidency. Since most people at the time were uneducated and were uninformed about government and campaigns (due largely to lack of communication), it seemed like a good idea._
  - _Many now believe the Electoral College is no longer needed. Most Americans of voting age can read and write, and TV and the Internet provide CONSTANT information about candidates and issues._)
- **EXTENSION:** This activity teaches basic information about the creation and workings of the Electoral College. For more in depth study, the student(s) could research arguments for and against the Electoral College and hold a debate about amending the Constitution to do away with it. An Internet search for "Electoral College debate" nets many interesting websites.

THE ELECTORAL COLLEGE

> The Electoral College actually elects the president every four years. The American people vote in November for electors who support their candidate. Then the electors representing the candidate with the most votes in each state meet in the Electoral College in December to vote. Article II, Section 1 of the Constitution lays out the details:
>
> The Electoral College:
> - Is made up of **electors** from U.S. states (538 at present).
> - The number of electors per state depends on population.
> - Each state gets the same number of electors as representatives in the House + 2 senators (For example, Missouri has 11 electors because it has 9 representative and 2 senators.)
> - Electors vote for the candidate that wins the most votes in their state.
> - A candidate needs 270 "electoral votes" to win the election.
> - In case of a tie, the House of Representatives votes to decide the new president.

Which of these sentences states the **MAIN IDEA** of the information?
  A. The Electoral College has more power than the American people.
  B. The Electoral College is elected to vote for the American president.
  C. The Electoral College cannot elect the same person the people do.
  D. The Electoral College is made up of 538 people from the 50 states.

The word "elector" **MOST NEARLY** means
  A. the group that elects the president every 4 years.
  B. House member who wants to join the Electoral College.
  C. a state representative who votes for the U.S. president.
  D. the person who wins the most votes for America's president.

Which sentence **BEST** explains the number of people in the Electoral College?
  A. People from all 50 states meet to elect the president.
  B. A candidate must win 270 electoral votes to become president.
  C. The Constitution says there should always be 538 electors.
  D. Each state's electors are equal to its members in the U.S. Congress.

Why do you think the founding fathers may have formed the Electoral College?

_____

_____

_____

THE ELECTORAL COLLEGE ANSWERS & EXPLANATIONS

The Electoral College actually elects the president every four years. The American people vote in November for electors who support their candidate. Then the electors representing the candidate with the most votes in each state meet in the Electoral College in December to vote. Article II, Section 1 of the Constitution lays out the details:

The Electoral College:

- Is made up of **electors** from U.S. states (538 at present).
- The number of electors per state depends on population.
- Each state gets the same number of electors as representatives in the House + 2 senators (For example, Missouri has 11 electors because it has 9 representative and 2 senators.)
- Electors vote for the candidate that wins the most votes in their state.
- A candidate needs 270 "electoral votes" to win the election.
- In case of a tie, the House of Representatives votes to decide the new president.

Which of these sentences states the **MAIN IDEA** of the information?
- A. The Electoral College has more power than the American people.
- B. The Electoral College is elected to vote for the American president. *
- C. The Electoral College cannot elect the same person the people do.
- D. The Electoral College is made up of 538 people from the 50 states.

(A and C are false, and D is a detail. Choice B summarizes the information.)

The word "elector" **MOST NEARLY** means
- A. the group that elects the president every 4 years.
- B. House member who wants to join the Electoral College.
- C. a state representative who votes for the U.S. president. *
- D. the person who wins the most votes for America's president.

(An elector is a person, not a group, and D is the leading presidential candidate. Choice B CAN be true, but does not state a definition; C does.)

Which sentence **BEST** explains the number of people in the Electoral College?
- A. People from all 50 states meet to elect the president.
- B. A candidate must win 270 electoral votes to become president.
- C. The Constitution says there should always be 538 electors.
- D. Each state's electors are equal to its members in the U.S. Congress. *

(Choice D paraphrases the third bullet point in the box.)

Why do you think the founding fathers may have formed the Electoral College?
Answers may vary and should prompt some discussion.

BACK in TIME

THE TIME: Don your powdered wigs to go "back in time" to the late 1700's when the Constitution was written.

THE PLACE: Few people in the United States attend school. Many either cannot read at all, or can barely do so. Most live on farms far from the large cities of Philadelphia, Boston, or others. Few get or read newspapers. They hear little news other than what goes on in their local communities.

Only a few people are highly educated. Many of them serve as leaders such as the founding fathers. These educated few will also serve as the first electors in the Electoral College. They are the ones who will really elect the president.

DIRECTIONS: You are a highly educated person and a member of the Electoral College. Read about people who have won the most votes for U.S. president. For each, tell what you will do and why.

Jonathan Money Bags traveled the country giving folks $1.00 each to vote for him for president. And he won the most votes in your state.

Will you vote for him? Why or why not? _____

_____

_____

Peter Promise-Maker said if he became president, he would hold a White House cook-out every Thursday of his term. The people in your state voted for him to enjoy the fun.

Will you vote for him? Why or why not? _____

_____

_____

Stephen Skilled is smart, educated, and has worked in government for many years. He was the leader of one of the largest colonies. Now he won your state's votes for president and plans to make the U.S. strong and rich.

Will you vote for him? Why or why not? _____

_____

_____

WHAT'S THE POINT?

Why do you think the founding fathers set up the Electoral College in the Constitution? _____

_____

_____

_____

_____

Do you agree with the founding fathers? Why or why not? _____

_____

_____

_____

_____

How is the United States different than it was when the Constitution was written?

_____

_____

_____

_____

_____

Do you think the Electoral College is still needed? Why or why not? Explain at least three reasons. _____

_____

_____

_____

_____

_____

_____

_____

_____

Outside Influences

Objective: The student will be able to explain the main role of interest groups.

Materials:
In Your Best Interest? (Springboard handout)
Very "Interest"-ing! (handout)

Terms to know:
interest group - those who try to sway government leaders to help their cause
acronym - formed by the first letters of the words in a full name
discrimination - poor treatment due to one's race, religion, etc.

Procedure:

· After reviewing the Springboard, explain that *in this lesson the student(s) will research some interest groups to learn what they do and why*.

· Either assign (from Springboard and other as desired) or let the student(s) chose a group of interest to research. Distribute the "Very "Interest"-ing!" note-taking form to guide their research.

· Have the student(s) work individually, in pairs, or small groups to conduct their research and complete the form.

· Have them share what they learned and discuss, using the note-taking questions as a guide.

 # In Your Best Interest?

DIRECTIONS: Read what each interest group does below to match each group with its purpose. Write the acronyms you think fit in each blank.

INTEREST GROUPS:

PETA (People for the Ethical Treatment of Animals)
NOW (National Organization for Women)
NAACP (National Association for the Advancement of Colored People)
AARP (American Association of Retired Persons)
NRA (National Rifle Association)
NEA (National Education Association)
AFL-CIO (American Federation of Labor and Congress of Industrial Organizations)
WGA (Writer's Guild of America)

_____ 1. Protects the rights of Americans to own guns.

_____ 2. Works to stop testing on animals in laboratories.

_____ 3. Tried to improve wages and working conditions.

_____ 4. Wants to help teachers and students succeed.

_____ 5. Works to end racial hatred and discrimination.

_____ 6. Takes action to bring about equality for females.

_____ 7. Represents people in the entertainment business.

_____ 8. Wants to protect the rights of elderly people.

What do you think is the main purpose for interest groups? How do you think they get the government to act in their "interest"? _____

_____

_____

_____

_____

Do you think interest groups are helpful to government and the people? Explain your ideas. _____

_____

_____

_____

_____

VERY "INTEREST"-ING!

Name of Group:

Website(s) studied:

Main Purpose/Cause they support:

Actions taken to further its cause:

How much power do you think the group has? Why?

Do you think this group is needed? Why or why not?

Springboard:
Students should study the "Levels of Government" handout and complete the ranking.
(From top down: U.S. Constitution, federal laws, state laws,
country laws, city laws.)

Objective: The student will be able to explain some issues that are handled by different levels of government.

Materials: Levels of Government (Springboard handout)
                        Issue cards (one cut-out set per student or pair)
                        Focus (1/2-page handout)

Terms to know: **issue** - problem or concern
                        tourism - travel for pleasure
                        veteran - someone who has served in the military

Procedure:
- After reviewing the Springboard, explain that *the U.S. Constitution outlines the federal or national government, but there are also governments at the state, city, town, county, and other levels (Different states call lower governments different names: parishes, townships, etc.). Many issues are dealt with by local and state governments.* (Review your local governments, what they're called and their specific names.)
- Have the student(s) work in pairs or with the instructor, giving each pair a set of "Issue Cards." Instruct the student(s) to *sort the cards based on the level of government (local, state or federal) they think would BEST handle or SHOULD handle the issues.*
- Issue-by-issue, have the student(s) share how they grouped each and their reasoning. *(Since many issues are addressed by two or more levels, any student groupings are fine, as long as they are well-reasoned. Tourists for example, visit towns, cities, states, and travel the nation.)*
- Then distribute the "Focus" handout, have the student(s) pick one issue as directed, and explain how all three levels of government address it. The student(s) can work individually, in pairs, or groups on this.)
  Have them share their ideas and discuss. *(Answers will vary, but in general the federal government gets more involved in the "big picture," while state and local governments deal with day–to day details. For example:*
  ○ *Issue: public schools*
  ○ *Local response: hiring teachers*
  ○ *State response: deciding what will be taught in science classes*
  ○ *Federal response: new national requirements to raise graduation rates.)*

Levels of Government

Most of this unity study has looked at the federal government. But cities, counties, and states also have governments. These do some of the same jobs as the federal government and some different jobs.

	Federal	State	Local
Executive Branch	President, Vice President, Cabinet, various Departments	Governor, Lieutenant Governor, Treasurer, Attorney, Departments	Mayor, County Administrator, Sheriff, Treasurer, Departments
Legislative Branch	Senate, House of Representatives, Library of Congress, Treasury, and other offices	State Senate, State House or General Assembly, Committees, Budget, and other offices	City or County Council or Commission, Boards of Health, Schools, etc.
Judicial Branch	Supreme Court, Federal Courts of Appeals, and others hearing National or International issues	State Supreme Court, State Courts of Appeals, and others hearing cases related to state issues or local issues on appeal	City and Traffic Courts hear cases about local issues

DIRECTIONS: Based on the chart and what you already know, write the laws below on the ladder. The most powerful goes at the top, and the least on the bottom rung.

State laws

City laws

U.S. Constitution

County laws

Federal laws

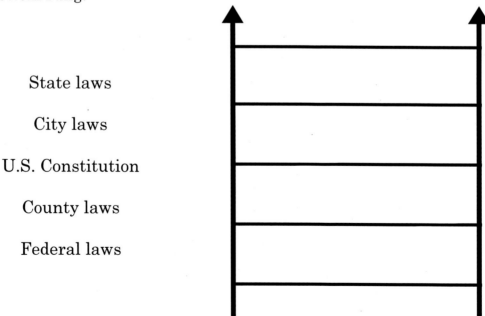

Issue Cards

Police Departments	The Army, Navy, Air Force, and Marines	Clean up after a Flood	Traffic Lights and Stop Signs
Building Prisons	Immigration Issues and Laws	Trade with Other Nations	Rules for Elections
Public Schools	State Parks	Child Day Care	Tourism
Money to Study and Cure Diseases	Garbage	Prices of Gas, Electric, Cable, Phone, etc.	Health Care
Fire Departments	Food for the Needy	Museums and Parks	School Uniforms
Planning City Roads	Loans for Small Businesses	Rules for Banking and Business	Voting Rights
Road Safety	The Environment	Numbers of People without Jobs	Building Bridges
Crime	Gun Laws	Taxes	Veterans' Care

DIRECTIONS: Pick one issue card you think is addressed by all three levels of government. Explain how each level could respond to the problem or issue.

Issue:
Federal Response:
State Response:
Local Response:

DIRECTIONS: Pick one issue card you think is addressed by all three levels of government. Explain how each level could respond to the problem or issue.

Issue:
Federal Response:
State Response:
Local Response:

Hit the Books

Objective: The student will be able to analyze a book to identify its main points.

Materials:
Past or Present? (Springboard handout)
"Primary Source" Planner (handout - see **NOTE**)
"Primary Source" Scoring (1/2-page rubric)

Terms to know:
primary source - visual or written account of event by someone there

Procedure:

· While reviewing the Springboard, make sure student(s) understand what primary sources are (see terms), and have them name examples from the unit. *(Primary sources include the U.S. Constitution, Articles of Confederation, Declaration of Independence, The Bill of Rights, etc.).* Go on to explain that *in this lesson the student(s) will create some "primary sources" from the books they read (as though they WERE there!).*

· (**NOTE:** Before distributing the "'Primary Source' Planner," fill in the number of sources you want to assign based upon student ability and available time.) Distribute the handout and review the various types of sources and requirements. Then allow time for the student(s) to plan and create their projects as directed.

· Have them share their sources and/or set up a "museum" for others to tour and read the descriptions. Have the student(s) evaluate their work using the "'Primary Source' Scoring" rubric.)

©InspirEd Educators, Inc.

PAST OR PRESENT?

DIRECTIONS: Tell if each thing is from a past time of study, a time closer to present, or if it both could be true. Be prepared to explain your ideas.

Diary entry by Thomas Jefferson -

A photograph of the founding fathers -

A textbook chapter on the Articles of Confederation -

A letter written by John Adams to his wife Abigail -

A newspaper story about the election of 1980 -

The U.S. Constitution -

A book about a founding father -

The pen used to sign the Declaration of Independence -

A magazine article about the 200th anniversary of the Constitution -

What do you think?

1. Which of these things do you think tells us the **MOST** about the past? Why?

2. Why do you think it is important to know when sources were written or made?

PAST OR PRESENT?
ANSWERS & EXPLANATIONS

DIRECTIONS: Tell if each thing is from a past time of study, a time closer to present, or if it both could be true. Be prepared to explain your ideas.

Diary entry by Thomas Jefferson - *The Past; it was written by a person from a time in history.*

A painting of the founding fathers - *Possibly both; if someone painted it while the men posed, it is from the past. If a more recent artist painted it using other images, it is from the present.*

A textbook chapter on the Articles of Confederation. - *Present; most textbooks are written by historians about a time in history.*

A letter written by John Adams to his wife Abigail - *The Past; John Adams would have been alive to write a letter to his wife!*

A newspaper story about the election of 1980 - *Possibly both; if it were written at that time, it is from the past. If it is a more recent article that looks back at that election, it would be considered present.*

The U.S. Constitution - *The Past; we know this document was written in 1787.*

A book about a founding father – *This COULD be both, but was most likely written by some later scholar ABOUT the founding father. While there may have been a book about him written during his lifetime, it is more likely from the present.*

The pen used to sign the Declaration of Independence - *The Past; it is an object from that time.*

A magazine article about the 200th anniversary of the Constitution - *The Present; it was written 200 years after the event.*

What do you think?
1. Which of these things do you think tells us the **MOST** about the past? Why?
Answers may vary and should be logically explained. Note that when something is written later by a person who was not there or even by someone who WAS, the account is affected by that person's views of the events or personal opinions. Even so, primary sources are what MOST scholars study to learn about past events, assuming that those closer to the time can give a clearer description.

2. Why do you think it is important to know when sources were written or made?
Answers may vary but should be justified and spark discussion.

JOIN, or DIE.

"PRIMARY SOURCE" PLANNER

DIRECTIONS: Create at least _____ "primary sources" from the time of the book you read that will help others understand some main points of the book. Explain in writing what each "primary source" is and its importance to the book. Write on index cards to tape to or near each source. Use this page to jot your ideas. Fill in the empty rows with any not listed. Remember, primary sources are writings or objects from the past, so try to make them look "real"!

Source	How if "Fits"/Explains Book	Making It Look "Real"
Diary or journal		
Letter / Other Writing		
Photo, drawing, etc.		
Document / Record		
Clothes, tools, etc.		

"Primary Source" Scoring

Use this scale to rate your work:

4- Excellent   3 - Good   2 - Fair   1- Poor   0 - Unacceptable

	Student	Teacher
Created assigned number of sources	_____	_____
Sources look "real"	_____	_____
Sources "fit" MAIN points in book	_____	_____
Clearly explained	_____	_____
Creative ideas	_____	_____
Spelling and grammar	_____	_____

GRADE:

COMMENTS:

"Primary Source" Scoring

Use this scale to rate your work:

4- Excellent   3 - Good   2 - Fair   1- Poor   0 - Unacceptable

	Student	Teacher
Created assigned number of sources	_____	_____
Sources look "real"	_____	_____
Sources "fit" MAIN points in book	_____	_____
Clearly explained	_____	_____
Creative ideas	_____	_____
Spelling and grammar	_____	_____

GRADE:

COMMENTS:

Reviewing Terms

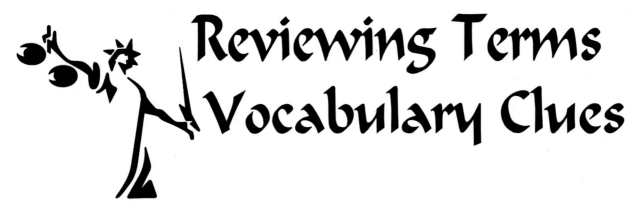

Reviewing Terms
Vocabulary Clues

ACROSS

3 those who seek to sway government action for their cause
6 problem or concern
8 change or add to
12 put into action
14 one in America under English rule
16 one who tells what they know in a trial
19 opening of the Constitution
20 forgive for a crime
22 large meeting
23 member of a state or nation
24 where facts of cases are heard and ruled upon
25 one running for office
26 break a law
29 changes to a document
33 formed by the first letters of words
37 agreement between nations
39 approve
41 one who has served in the military
42 statement of main ideas
44 group that elects the president
45 members of the Supreme Court
46 skill, etc. needed to do a job
47 account of past event by someone who was there
48 delegate at the Electoral College

DOWN

1 hearing to decide court cases
2 rule and control of a country
4 written plan for a new law
5 the right to look at lower court rulings to see that they violate the Constitution
7 poor treatment due to one's race
9 say "no" as to a law
10 for a whole nation
11 plan of government
13 travel for fun
15 group with common ideas that works to elect candidates
17 charge and try for crimes in office
18 number of people in a place
21 leaders of early America
27 group of people chosen to decide cases
28 one who speaks/votes for others
30 the world around us
31 money paid to the government
32 not a Republican or a Democrat
34 representative at a convention
35 freedom
36 body of law makers
38 important piece of writing
40 ask for another trial
43 army, navy, air force, etc.

Reviewing Terms Puzzle Answers

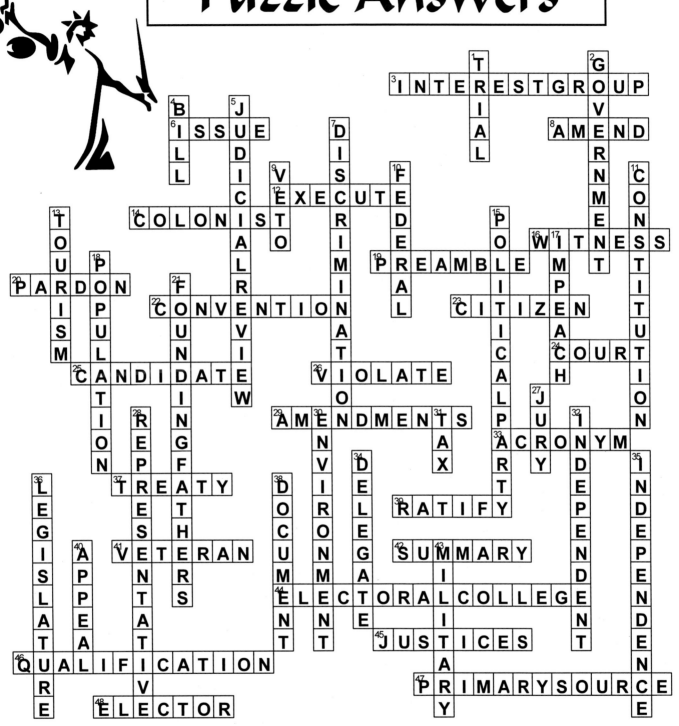

Across and Down answers:

1. TRIAL
2. GOVERNMENT
3. INTEREST GROUP
4. BILL
5. JUDICIAL REVIEW
6. ISSUE
7. DISCRIMINATION
8. AMEND
9. VETO
10. FEDERAL
11. CONSTITUTION
12. EXECUTE
13. TOURISM
14. COLONIST
15. POLITICAL PARTY
16. WITNESS
17. IMPEACH
18. POPULATION
19. PREAMBLE
20. PARDON
21. FUNDING
22. CONVENTION
23. CITIZEN
24. COURT
25. CANDIDATE
26. VIOLATE
27. JURY
28. REPRESENTATIVES
29. AMENDMENTS
30. ENVIRONMENT
31. TAX
32. INDEPENDENT
33. ACRONYM
34. DELEGATE
35. INDEPENDENCE
36. LEGISLATURE
37. TREATY
38. DOCUMENT
39. RATIFY
40. APPEA
41. VETERAN
42. SUMMARY
43. MILITARY
44. ELECTORAL COLLEGE
45. JUSTICES
46. QUALIFICATION
47. PRIMARY SOURCE
48. ELECTOR

Matching - Write the letter of the correct answer in the blank:

_____	1. government	A.	someone running for office
_____	2. tax	B.	agreement between two or more countries
_____	3. legislature	C.	member of the Supreme Court
_____	4. bill	D.	rule and control of a country
_____	5. treaty	E.	one who served in the military
_____	6. appeal	F.	a law making body
_____	7. justice	G.	the world around us
_____	8. environment	H.	written plan for a new law
_____	9. candidate	I.	ask for a new trial
_____	10. veteran	J.	money paid to the government

Give an example of each:

11. tax - _____

12. document - _____

13. political party - _____

14. court - _____

15. primary source - _____

Multiple Choice - Write the letter of the correct answer in the blank:

16._____ Which part of the Constitution tells its purpose?
    A. Article I, Section I   C. the Preamble
    B. The Amendments   D. The Bill of Rights

17._____ The first ten amendments to the U.S. Constitution are called the
    A. Constitutional Convention.   C. Bill of Rights.
    B. Declaration of Independence.   D. Supreme Court.

18._____ The job of the Electoral College is to
    A. write amendments.   C. approve state judges.
    B. protect Senators.   D. elect the president.

19._____ Voting, serving on juries, and working in government are all examples of
    A. good citizenship.   C. checks and balances.
    B. judicial review.   D. government powers.

Fully answer the question:
20. Explain how a bill becomes a law.

*The **media** is very important to today's elections. Most people learn of events and get information from these sources. In the past, few people kept up with what happened in their world. Even if they had newspapers, most people could not read them or at least not very well.*

Today information is easy to get and understand. The changes in the media have also changed elections. Candidates today must be very careful what they say and do. A news reporter or camera is almost always nearby! How the media presents information also makes a difference. Reporters can "spin" stories, or present facts in ways that can sway people's views. And this spin can change the way people vote for a candidate or issue.

21. _____ Which "media" would be **LEAST LIKELY** to affect elections?
    A. the Internet   C. TV news
    B. newspapers   D. movies

22. _____ What is the **MAIN IDEA** of the reading?
    A. Candidates are often followed by reporters.
    B. The media has changed today's elections.
    C. We now live in an "information age."
    D. Elections were fairer in the past.

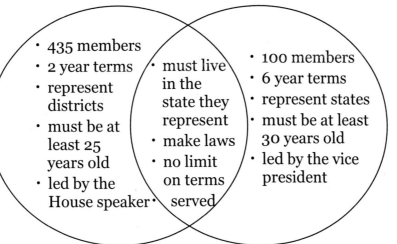

23. ____ This graphic is a
    A. Venn diagram.   C. bar graph.
    B. primary source.   D. pie chart.

24. ____ The graphic compares the
    A. two houses of the U.S. Congress.
    B. powers of state and local governments.
    C. duties of the president and vice president.
    D. executive, legislative, and judicial branches.

25. ____ Which sentence tells how the two are similar?
    A. There are more members in one than the other.
    B. Members must live in the state they represent.
    C. The speaker and the vice president lead both.
    D. Ages for members are different, 25 and 30.

Fill in the blanks with unit terms:
1. Americans living under English rule were known as _____.
2. The nation's government plan is its _____.
3. Some laws require people to pay _____ to the government.
4. _____ are added to make changes to the Constitution.
5. The city has a _____ of over two million people.
6. Every U.S. _____ has the right to free speech.
7. Members of the Supreme Court are called _____.
8. The _____`_____ includes members of the army and navy.
9. A/An _____ hears facts of a case and must agree on a verdict.
10. USA is a/an _____ for the United States of America.

Give an example of each:
11. founding father - _____
12. document - _____
13. political party - _____
14. interest group - _____
15. issue - _____

Multiple Choice – Write the letter of the correct answer in the blank:
16. _____ The Articles of Confederation were weak because the
    A. federal government was weaker than the states.
    B. president was able to serve too many terms in office.
    C. states were unable to collect taxes from citizens.
    D. power was divided among branches of government.

17. _____ Electors are chosen to
    A. ratify laws passed by Congress.
    B. help the Supreme Court decide its rulings.
    C. represent their states in the U.S. Senate.
    D. meet and vote for the United States president.

18. _____ The system of checks and balances was created to
    A. allows laws to be made faster and more fairly.
    B. outline what the role of government should be.
    C. ensure no one branch of government became too powerful.
    D. allow the Constitution to be changed to adapt to new times.

19. _____ The **MOST** important power of Congress is
    A. impeachment of the president.
    B. helping interest groups.
    C. making laws for the nation.
    D. judicial review of laws.

Fully answer on your own paper and attach:
20. Briefly explain the process to amend the Constitution

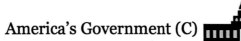

Fill in the blanks with unit terms:

1. Bill is to the phone company, as _____ is to the government.
2. Local is to city, as national is to _____.
3. Inventor is to a machine, as _____ is to our government.
4. Right and write are homonyms, as USA is to_____.
5. Judges are to lower courts, as _____ are to the Supreme Court.
6. Turn down is to refuse, as approve is to _____.
7. Sign is to approve, as return a bill unsigned is to _____.
8. Architect's drawing is to house, as _____ is to government.
9. Introduction is to a story, as _____ is to the Constitution.
10. Business travel is to meetings, as _____ is to vacations.

Name each grouping with a unit term:

11. army, navy, air force - _____
12. Congress, Senate, House of Representatives - _____
13. Bill of Rights, president's term, alcohol sales - _____
14. arrest, right to a lawyer, fair trial - _____
15. global warming, gun rights, protecting the environment - _____

Multiple Choice – Write the letter of the correct answer in the blank:

16. _____ The Articles of Confederation were changed because
    A. the federal government was too weak to govern the nation.
    B. it divided power among the three branches of government.
    C. states needed money and couldn't collect their own taxes.
    D. the president was able to serve too many terms in office.

17. _____ The Electoral College was formed to
    A. ratify laws passed by the U.S. Congress.
    B. help the Supreme Court decide which cases to hear.
    C. ensure free and fair election of U.S. presidents.
    D. represent their states in the House of Representatives

18. _____ Which sentence gives an example of checks and balances?
    A. Senators serve six-year terms; the president makes treaties.
    B. The president issues executive orders; Congress levies taxes.
    C. Congress makes laws; Supreme Court members serve for life.
    D. The President is commander-in-chief; Congress declares war.

19. _____ Which person or group has the FINAL say about laws?
    A. Congress   C. Supreme Court
    B. the president   D. Speaker of the House

Fully answer on your own paper and attach:

20. Why do you think some powers are given to states and some to the federal government? Explain your ideas.

95

Form A:

1. D
2. J
3. F
4. H
5. B
6. I
7. C
8. G
9. A
10. E

11. sales tax, income tax, tax on clothes, etc.
12. U.S. Constitution, Declaration of Independence, etc.
13. Republican, Democrat, Green Party, etc.
14. Supreme, Appeals, state, etc.
15. diary, letter, photograph, etc.
16. C
17. C
18. D
19. A
20. A bill is must pass both houses of Congress in the same form. If it does, it goes to the president, who either ratifies it to become a law or vetoes it.

Form B:

1. colonists
2. constitution
3. taxes
4. Amendments
5. population
6. citizen
7. justices
8. military
9. jury (court)
10. acronym

11. Thomas Jefferson, Washington,, Ben Franklin, etc.
12. U.S. Constitution, Declaration of Independence, etc.
13. Republican, Democrat, Green Party, etc.
14. PETA, NOW, AARP, etc.
15. global warming, health care, gun rights, etc.
16. A
17. D
18. C
19. C
20. Amendments must pass by (2/3 of) both houses of Congress. They are then sent to the state legislatures. If ¾ of the states ratify the amendment, it is added to the Constitution.

Form C:

1. tax
2. federal
3. founding father
4. (an) acronym
5. justices
6. ratify
7. veto
8. constitution
9. Preamble
10. tourism

11. military
12. legislature
13. amendments
14. due process
15. issues
16. A
17. C
18. D
19. C
20. Answers may vary but should make sense. Possible ideas include: to allow people more say by keeping some powers closer to home; to balance the power of the federal government and keep it from becoming too powerful, etc.

Skills for Forms A-C:

21. D
22. B
23. A
24. A
25. B

RESOURCES

www.usa.gov/ - The U.S. Government's Official Web Portal, U.S. General Services Administration, 2010.

www.thisnation.com/ - ThisNation.com – American Government & Politics on line, 2008.

www.whitehouse.gov - The White House official website, 2010.

bensguide.gpo.gov/ - Ben's Guide to U.S. Government for Kids, Superintendent of Documents, U.S. Government Printing Office, 2010.

www.crf-usa.org/ - The Constitutional Rights Foundation website.

www.youthforjustice.org/state.html - Youth for Justice, 2006.

www.politics1.com - "Politics 1: The Ultimate Guide to U.S. Politics and Elections Since 1997," Politics1, Ron Gunzburger, 2010.

www.census.gov/compendia/statab/elections - "Elections," The National Data Book, U.S. Census Bureau, 2010.

justvote.org - "Register to Vote," JustVote.org, Just Vote, 2010.

www.ourdocuments.gov/doc.php?flash=true&doc=3 - "Articles of Confederation," Our Documents.gov, National Archives and Records Administration, 2010.

www.rockingham.k12.va.us/JFHMS/principles.htm - "Fundamental Principles of American Government," Rockingham County Public Schools, 2010.

www.law.cornell.edu/constitution/constitution.overview.html - "The Constitution of the United States of America," Legal Information Institute, Cornell University, 2010.

www.usconstitution.net/const.html#Amends - "The Amendments," U.S. Constitution, Steve Mount, 2010.

www.fairvote.org - FairVote.org, 2010.

www.usconstitution.net/constamnotes.html - "Notes on the Amendments," The U.S. Constitution Online, 2010.

www.democrats.com - The Official Homepage of the Democratic National Committee.

www.republicans.com - The Official Homepage of the Republican National Committee.

www.archives.gov/federal-register/electoral-college/index.html - "U.S. Electoral College," National Archives and Records Administration, 2010.

www.time.com/time/election2004/article/0,18471,749496,00.html#Anchor-top - Dell, Kristina, "The Electoral College Explained," Time.com,, 2004.

www.archives.gov/presidential-libraries/contact/libraries.html - "Presidential Libraries," The National Archives homepage, 2010.

www.crf-usa.org/ - The Constitutional Rights Foundation website, 2010.

www.govspot.com/ - U.S. Government, State Government, Congress, Government Jobs and more, 2010.

www.enchantedlearning.com/vote/presidential_elections.html - "How the President of the United States Is Elected," Enchanted Learning.com, Enchanted Learning, 2010.

www.supremecourtus.gov/about/briefoverview.pdf - "A Brief Overview of the Supreme Court," About the Supreme Court, Supreme Court US.gov, 2010.

www.oyez.org - OYEZ: U.S. Supreme Court Media, The Oyez Project, 2009.

www.landmarkcases.org/ - "Landmark Supreme Court Cases," Landmark Cases.org, Street Law and the Supreme Court Historical Society, 2002.

www.law.cornell.edu/supct/cases/topic.htm - "Historic Supreme Court Decisions by Topic," Cornell University Law School, 2009.

www.senate.gov/general/contact_information/senators_cfm.cfm - "Senators by State," Senate.gov, U.S. Senate, 2010.

www.congress.org/congressorg/directory/congdir.tt?action=myreps_form -"Write Your Officials" and "Congressional Directory," Congress.org, Capitol Advantage, LLC, 2010.

www.usconstitution.net/consttop_law.html - "Constitutional Topic: How a Bill Becomes a Law," The U.S. Constitution Online, Steve Mount, 2010.

www.civiced.org/ - Center for Civic Education, 2010.

www.earlyamerica.com/earlyamerica/freedom/ - America's Freedom Documents, 2010.